Impeccable Connections

—The Rise and Fall of Richard Whitney

Brick Tower Press
Habent Sua Fata Libelli

Brick Tower Press
1230 Park Avenue
New York, New York 10128
Tel: 212-427-7139
bricktower@aol.com • www.BrickTowerPress.com

Library of Congress Cataloging-in-Publication Data
MacKay, Malcolm
Impeccable Connections
Includes biographical references and footnotes
ISBN 978-1-883283-62-9

1. Whitney, Richard— 2. Business—United States 3. Biography—
Business Leaders 4. Business—New York Stock Exchange

Impeccable Connections

—The Rise and Fall of Richard Whitney

Malcolm MacKay

ACKNOWLEDGMENTS

While I am grateful to many people who graciously assisted me in writing this book, I would like to mention five specifically. My wife Julia was a constant source of encouragement and editorial insight, not to mention spelling (not one of my strengths). Sara Faison brought her considerable editorial skills to the project. Jim Grant couldn't have been more supportive. Caroline Anderson served as photographic archivist, and I only wish we could have reproduced all her discoveries. I have worked for many happy years with Nancy MacDougall, who did yeoman's service at the keyboard.

Table of Contents

" NOT DICK WHITNEY. NOT DICK WHITNEY. "

—Franklin D. Roosevelt
upon being told Richard Whitney
was a criminal

This photograph of Richard Whitney was taken at his lawyer's office on March 9, 1938, the day after the scandal became public. Note the ever-present Porcellian Club charm on the watch chain.

PREFACE

The Roaring Twenties were never louder than at the southwest corner of Wall and Broad, home of the New York Stock Exchange, especially as summer turned into fall in 1929. The Dow Industrial Average, 63.90 eight years earlier, rose to 381.17 on September 3, 1929, a record high that would stand for the next quarter century. The next few weeks were marked by unusual price volatility, culminating on Wednesday, October 23, with unprecedented trading volume. This was also the day the Chrysler Building surpassed the Eiffel Tower in height, making it—briefly—the tallest man-made structure in the world.

Neither the Exchange's president nor vice president, both unpaid, part-time positions back then, were in town that day. The president was on his honeymoon in Hawaii, and the vice president, Richard Whitney, was serving as a steward—or judge—at the annual Essex Fox Hounds steeplechase races in Far Hills, New Jersey. As master of the hunt, Whitney spoke with authority as he declared one race a dead heat and determined fault in another during which two contestants had collided.

The next day, October 24, has gone down in history as Black Thursday. Prices collapsed from the opening bell. Winston Churchill, who happened to be in the visitors' gallery, looked on with amazement at the chaos on the trading floor. A large, silent crowd gathered on the street outside. An air of panic grew in direct proportion to the stock ticker falling further and further behind.

Would the cavalry come to the rescue? As the Trinity Church bells rang out at noon, several well-known bankers worked their way through the crowd and entered 23 Wall Street, the unmarked offices of J. P.

Morgan & Co., the Morgan bank. The bankers soon left, and Morgan's senior partner, Tom Lamont, met the press. "There has been a little distress selling on the Stock Exchange," he said, "and we have held a meeting of the heads of several financial institutions to discuss the situation." Frederick Lewis Allen would call that one of the most remarkable understatements of all time.

At one thirty, representing the bankers who had earlier met with Lamont, Richard Whitney, acting president of the Exchange and Morgan's primary bond broker, strode onto the trading floor. He was forty-one years old, over six feet tall, and exquisitely dressed in a three-piece suit with a watch chain displaying the gold pig charm of Harvard's exclusive Porcellian Club. His presence caused the traders on the floor to freeze. All eyes turned to him and no one spoke. Described by observers as debonair, confident, determined, even jaunty, he went directly to the US Steel specialist, offering $205—the last sale price, but well above the current offering price—for ten thousand shares. He proceeded to other trading posts, bidding for other blue chip stocks, also at the price of the last sale.

Whitney's intervention, resulting in over twenty million dollars in orders, arrested the panic. By day's end, the market was off only twelve points. As one newspaper's headline put it the next day, "Richard Whitney Halts Stock Panic." Prices held fairly firm on Friday and Saturday, only to collapse the next week absent any additional support from the angel bankers.

Although the success of Whitney's intervention was fleeting, he emerged as something of a heroic figure. Elected president of the Exchange the following spring, he would be reelected four times and become the national spokesman for the Exchange, as well as for the securities industry generally. He often testified in Washington, spoke to business groups around the country, and appeared in news clips shown at movie houses. CBS and NBC carried his speeches on national radio. In 1934, he appeared on the cover of *Time* magazine.

Whitney's message was clear: the securities industry could regulate itself, and the federal government should stay out. He led the industry's opposition to the Securities Act of 1933, which imposed disclosure requirements on the industry, and the Securities Exchange Act of 1934, which created the Securities Exchange Commission as the regulatory agency for the industry. Whitney brooked no compromise. There was even talk of him becoming the Republican presidential candidate to run against Franklin Roosevelt in 1936.

Things were not, however, as they appeared. While the public Whitney flourished, the private Whitney self-destructed. He lived beyond his means, he invested terribly, he borrowed more and more, he stole securities that had been entrusted to him. Flash forward to March 1938, and we find him being booked at the Elizabeth Street police station for the embezzlement of funds. He admits everything and assumes sole responsibility for his acts. Simon Breen, the police lieutenant behind the desk, says, "Mr. Whitney, I'm sorry to see you in this trouble and I wish you luck." "Thank you," replies Whitney, and they shake hands. A photographer standing behind the officer takes a photograph of Whitney, in a dark suit with the ever-present Porcellian charm on his watch chain. The charm reflects the bright light from the flashbulb, creating the impression of a large star.

My father once said that, with the exception of the Japanese attack on Pearl Harbor, the most shocking thing he had ever heard was that Richard Whitney was a crook. Others had similar reactions. According to Nancy Randolph, the society columnist for *The Daily News*, "Not in our time, in our father's time, nor in our grandfather's time has there been such a social debacle...He had no need to overreach himself for power, for money, or for social position. He has them all."

Time, in the issue after the arrest, observed, "The terrible thing about the Whitney scandal is...that the broker was the White Knight of the financial district. Whitney was Sir Richard when he went into battle in shining armor against the 1929 crash and again when he stood up and defied Washington and the reformers. Now it turns out that this Great White Knight was an optical illusion..."

My closest childhood friend, who died in a car accident his freshman year at Harvard, was Richard Whitney's grandson. From my friend's death in 1960 until Whitney's own fourteen years later, we kept in regular touch, abetted by the fact that he lived his final years literally down the road from my in-laws in Far Hills, New Jersey. I felt considerable affection for both him and Mrs. Whitney, who never flagged in her support for her husband. Arriving at my engagement party in 1963, Whitney grabbed my hand in his two and said, "I want to thank you, Malcolm. This is the first time I have been in society since my troubles." I have thought about Richard Whitney, and why he did what he did, all my life. This book tells his story.

THE FAMILY TREE

In the novel *This Side of Paradise*, Amory Blaine, Scott Fitzgerald's stand-in, is shocked to discover that the most "breathlessly aristocratic" member of his Princeton class is actually the son of a grocery store clerk who struck it rich in Tacoma real estate. There is a bit of this with the Whitneys. As Richard's great niece put it, "Our family always considered the Whitneys' side to have come from nothing."

Although very distant relatives included Eli Whitney, inventor of the cotton gin, and William Whitney, one of the builders of the New York City subway system, the direct American line from English immigrant John to Richard—eight generations—is one of hardscrabble Yankee farmers, sailors, and traders. If in old Boston the Lowells spoke only to the Cabots, and the Cabots only to God, there would have been no exception for the Whitneys. They were more Calvin Coolidge than Henry Cabot Lodge.

Countless descriptions to the contrary notwithstanding, John Whitney did not arrive on the *Arabella*, the Winthrop ship with the Pilgrims' most fashionable passenger list. He came five years later—1635—on the *Elizabeth and Ann*. A tailor by trade, he settled in Watertown, just up the Charles River from Cambridge, where the family remained for several generations. In 1666, John's son Thomas was awarded an annual stipend of thirty shillings to keep dogs out of the meetinghouse.

Richard Whitney's great-grandfather Elisha, born in 1747, was the first in Richard's line to leave Watertown. When not at sea, he lived in Beverly, a busy port just north of Boston known during the Revolution for its privateers who attacked British merchant ships. Originally a schoolteacher, Elisha became a ship's surgeon, albeit without a medical education or physician license, as the former barely existed at the time and the latter existed not at all. He sailed on ships under two Beverly captains, and amputated the leg of one so successfully that he was awarded with a chalice stolen at sea from a British ship and originally intended for the Governor of Barbados.

During the Revolution, Elisha was captured by the British, imprisoned in Halifax, and exchanged for a loyal subject of the crown. Family records raise the possibility that, as an advocate for inoculation against smallpox, he may have lost one of his children as a result of following his own advice.

Richard's grandfather Israel was born in Beverly in 1797, the second of Elisha's sons to be given that name. The first was among four of eleven siblings to die in infancy. Israel went to sea as a young man, and became captain of a merchant ship owned by a wealthy Beverly resident. He became famous locally in 1827 when his ship burned at sea. To quote from *The Beverly Citizen* at the time, his "heroic efforts to save the burning ship, his coolness and bravery, and his great suffering from exposure in an open boat at sea for many days will be long remembered."

According to a family history, Israel was once imprisoned in Algiers on piracy charges, and, upon release, walked across a desert to obtain ransom for his compatriots. After retiring from the sea, he was involved with several manufacturing companies and served as a cotton agent and as treasurer of a Lowell mill.

Keeping with family tradition, Israel had many children—twelve, in fact, of whom ten survived into adulthood. The third child, George— Richard's father—was born in Lowell in 1832. As a young man— starting at least by age seventeen, according to the Beverly census of 1850—he clerked in the office of an East India merchant and then formed his own trading company with a partner. He next joined his several brothers in another trading company and actually moved to Calcutta for several years.

Married at age thirty, George was widowed two years later and didn't remarry for almost two decades. With his second wife, he had a daughter and two sons, George and Richard. By the time of Richard's birth in Beverly Farms (adjoining Beverly) in August 1888, George (the father) had become president of a small Boston bank—North National Union.

As noted earlier, George was the third of Israel's children, but mention should be made of the youngest (by twenty-three years), Edward. It was Edward, Richard's uncle, who was the first in the Whitney line to move much beyond the Watertown-Beverly-Lowell triangle, and become a true member of the American financial and social establishment.

Edward, perhaps benefiting from his late birth order and coincidentally better family finances, attended Harvard, graduating in the class of 1871. The college, even as compared with others at the time, was a provincial institution. Of the 157 members of Edward's class to graduate, thirty-five were from Boston and fifty-six from elsewhere in Massachusetts. Fifty-five were Unitarian, twenty-five Congregational (called Orthodox in the class book), and thirty-two Episcopalian. Only five were Catholic, and none Jewish. At graduation, fifty-six planned to enter the law, by far the leading career choice.

Soon after graduation, Edward moved to Calcutta to join his brothers in their importing business, and he remained in India for twenty years. When he returned to Boston in 1891, he took a job as personal assistant to Jacob C. Rogers, who represented locally both the London firm of Pierpont Morgan's father and Pierpont Morgan's New York firm. In 1900, following Roger's death, Edward moved to New York as a Morgan partner.

The timing was perfect. The Morgan firm was at the height of its trust-creating powers, as witnessed by the formation of United States Steel the year after Edward's arrival. By 1906, Edward was able to build a country place on Long Island's North Shore, a favorite location for the Morgan crowd. Situated along the beach on Cove Neck in Oyster Bay, it was known for its extensive gardens, designed in a mixed classical and naturalistic style by a niece of Edith Wharton, the fashionable landscape architect Beatrix Farrand. Among a great many other examples of Farrand's work are the gardens at Dumbarton Oaks in Washington and the Otto Kahn estate on Long Island. Edward commuted to Wall Street on his steam yacht *Arrow*, 132 feet long and holder in the early twentieth century of the boat speed record of 45.6 miles per hour. Edward, like his nephews George and Richard was not one to hide his success.

Thus began the Whitney connection with Morgan. Richard's older brother George would follow his Uncle Edward to the firm, and eventually come to head it. A second and third generation would follow. It was Edward who would lend Richard, age twenty-three, the money to buy a seat on the New York Stock Exchange. Not long after, Richard became the principal bond broker for Morgan.

BECOMING BRAHMIN

The *Wall Street Journal* columnist Amity Shlaes, comparing Whitney and the Wall Street of his era with Bernard Madoff and today's financial world, noted:

> *Whitney sprang from the original American clan, that of the white Anglo-Saxon Protestant. Then, as now, there were also clans within the clan. It wasn't sufficient to be a Harvard alumnus. You also had to have attended the right school before that. Or sport the gold pig of Harvard's Porcellian Club. Or have important family connections to Wall Street leaders.*

Whitney was born with the advantages of American Protestant ancestors and an uncle who, albeit at age fifty, had become a Morgan partner. His family was comfortable financially, but not wealthy. His father was a self-made man. Whitney was well positioned to acquire the other membership indicia of the clan within the clan.

First, there was the village where Richard and his brother George spent their boyhood. Beverly Farms, just up the coast from Beverly itself, looked at the time of Richard's birth like a piece of rural England tucked away in the Massachusetts hills north of Boston. In fact, the area was really in transition from its struggling Calvinist past to its place as an Episcopalian country seat of Boston's Industrial Revolution gentry. The poet Oliver Wendell Holmes Sr., summered there, as did Henry Clay Frick. A century later, resident John Updike would write about the area in *Toward the End of Time*. In nearby South Hamilton, the Myopia Hunt

Club, still going strong today with its fox hunt and "the oldest continually running polo field" in the country, gives further evidence of the Anglophilia of America's patrician class.

In his Harvard twenty-fifth reunion book, Whitney listed riding, sailing, and tennis as favorite sports. These choices would fit with Beverly Farms, as would a sense of one's social eminence. Harland Davis, who would be chairman of the committee on business conduct of the New York Stock Exchange when Whitney was exposed, knew both Richard and George as boys, and years later recalled that he had taken an instant dislike to them as "perfect snobs" and "pains in the neck." Of course, the word snob derives from *sine nobilitate*—without nobility.

The observation that both Whitney boys were snobs would be repeated throughout their lives. The son of a Morgan partner of the 1930s remembered his father railing against both brothers' high-handedness in dealing with others. Maybe then-Senator Harry Truman captured this Whitney style best as it relates to George when he wrote his wife Bess the following shortly after becoming chairman of the Senate Banking Committee: "Mr. Whitney is very much inclined to feel his position. He came to my office…and told me what he was going to do. I simply asked him who the chairman of the committee happened to be."

Several miles to the west of Beverly Farms, just four years before Richard's birth, Endicott Peabody, a young Episcopal minister educated in England, founded a boarding school that both Richard and his older brother George would attend. He named it Groton, after the village on whose outskirts it sat. Endicott Peabody's father had worked for Pierpont Morgan's father in London. A founding trustee of the school, Pierpont donated the land on which it was built. Endicott Peabody's brother had married into the mill-owning Lawrence family, giving Peabody—and thus Groton—access to the wealthy of Boston. The Lawrences summered at Campobello with the James Roosevelts and their son Franklin, who became part of the New York delegation at Groton.

New great wealth wanted into the new school. For example, W. Averell Harriman was two years behind Richard Whitney at Groton. The son of the self-made railroad magnate joined the board of his father's Union Pacific Railroad while still in college. From the very beginning, and by conscious design, Groton was a most fashionable school.

The Episcopal boarding schools, of which St. Paul's School, founded in 1856 and located in Concord, New Hampshire, and Groton, are leading exemplars, represent a very different model from the older village academies—Exeter, Andover, Deerfield, Milton—that were really public schools before such things existed. The church schools, with buildings tucked near a chapel away from the center of town, attracted families whose social and recreational style was all about replicating English aristocratic life in America.

Groton admitted a few scholarship students, mostly clergymen's sons. Dean Acheson was the first of these. Acheson disliked the school, fought conformity, and graduated last, out of twenty-four, in his form in 1911. His grade average was sixty-eight. Peabody wrote Mrs. Acheson that he had failed to make "a Groton boy" of her son, to which she replied that she wanted an educated son, not a Groton boy. It must have surprised Peabody when his failed student, after a brilliant legal and governmental career, became Secretary of State.

In his diary, Peabody wrote that his purpose in founding Groton was "to cultivate manly Christian character, having regard to the moral and physical as well as the intellectual development." Character trumps brilliance. Sports teach leadership. No one from Groton or St. Paul's would have disputed Wellington's contention that Waterloo was won on the playing fields of Eton.

Samuel Drury, the longtime rector of St. Paul's, worried about his students: "...most of them at least one or two generations removed from manual labor. They are getting soft." Young men of privilege should play hard and resist creature comforts. At Groton, boys lived in cubicles about sixty square feet in area, with a bed, dresser, and chair. Cubicle walls were higher than boys' height, but stopped well short of the ceiling. In the communal lavatory the water only ran cold. After morning chapel, classes ran from 8:30 a.m. to noon, and then again for two periods in the afternoon. Next came sports, a second chapel service, dinner, and study hall. The Reverend and Mrs. Peabody bid every boy good night. In Whitney's time, a little more than one hundred students were enrolled at Groton, most arriving in first form—seventh grade—and graduating six years later.

Well liked by both faculty and students, Richard Whitney was a great success at Groton. His last year, he was junior prefect (student body vice president), captain of the baseball team, and sometimes acting football captain. He managed the school play, and served as treasurer (a position he would hold at several organizations) of the school camp for underprivileged boys.

Reading Peabody's sermons and letters, one is struck by how much value he placed on public service. He repeatedly would mention old Groton boys who had become, for example, ambassadors or bishops. This was a post-commercial perspective; there were no cheers for the market man. There was also a sense of New England exceptionalism; the Puritans had come to create a city of God, superior morally and otherwise to the wicked old world. As Russell Shorto points out in *The Island at the Center of the World*, the Puritans were "rooted in intolerance" and saw their religion and political views as "divinely anointed." New Amsterdam (later New York) offered a very different value system: secular, diverse, and opportunistic.

In *Old Money*, Nelson W. Aldrich Jr. noted the importance of friendships among the sons of the privileged. "These friendships were one of the deliberate objectives of Endicott Peabody in founding Groton." Again, Aldrich: "To belong to the Porcellian Club it was not enough—it still isn't—that one be friends with a member. One has to have been friends with him always, and in that elusive past perfect tense of the verb *to be* the socially ambitious read their sad fate."

Peabody's emphasis on the development of friendship among his students derived from his admiration of the cohesion and sense of self-defining community of the graduates of the great English public (private in our terminology) schools. Central to this community was the gentleman's code of conduct, with personal honesty being a preeminent value. As Shlaes put it in describing Whitney's social circle, "The closer someone was to the club's center, the more trustworthy he was deemed to be." Above all, a gentleman was honest.

Given his explicit goal of "forming" his students, Peabody was certainly an influential figure in the lives of many Groton graduates. The school's most prominent alumnus, Franklin D. Roosevelt, form of 1900, wrote from the White House to Peabody (who, incidentally, voted for Herbert Hoover in 1932):

More than forty years ago you said, in a sermon in the old Chapel, something about not losing boyhood ideals in later life. These were Groton ideals—taught by you—I try not to forget—and your words are still with me and with the hundreds of others of us boys.

It is ironic that Groton old-boy Roosevelt, who in the 1930s was seen by many as a traitor to his class, actually may have been its—and capitalism's—savior. Meanwhile, it was Richard Whitney, seen as the poster boy for (to quote Aldrich in a different context) "...that segment of the upper class which flourished on the Eastern Seaboard, and which has occupied the most prominent place in America's social imagination," who let his class down. The extraordinary shock many felt upon learning of Whitney's crimes was partly about his failure to live up to the gentleman's values he supposedly represented, values—particularly honesty—that were seen as justification for the class's advantages and even existence.

Endicott Peabody never gave up on Whitney. He would visit old boys, including Roosevelt in the White House, and he made no exception for Whitney in Sing Sing. During one visit, Whitney, who played on the prison school baseball team, asked Peabody for a right-handed first baseman's mitt (he was left-handed). When criticized for such visits, Peabody's response was direct: "He [Whitney] did wrong, but he has paid the penalty. He needs help and friendship and is entitled to a fresh start." At the time of sentencing, Peabody wrote the probation officer of Whitney's "distinguished ability and excellent character."

Although a few Grotonians detoured to Princeton, Yale, or elsewhere, the main road out of the school led to Harvard. Richard took it, as brother George had three years before. Between 1906 and 1932, 405 boys from Groton applied to Harvard, and all but three were accepted. The college of Whitney's time, as it was in his Uncle Edward's after the Civil War, was strikingly local. Of the 434 graduates in Whitney's class of 1911, 219 were born in Massachusetts and fifty-two in New York. Academically, Harvard was hardly demanding. Dean Byron Hurlbut noted in the college's 1911 annual report that students during the previous year had averaged more than thirty class absences apiece.

Whitney rowed on the 1909 crew that beat Yale, and served as treasurer of the Hasty Pudding Club, a student theater group. His academic record was undistinguished. Years later, he would say that he had no interest in abstract ideas, but only in practical and tangible ones. Like many students from strong secondary schools, he was given advanced placement credit and completed the required course work early. Unlike some in this situation, including FDR, he chose to leave college once he had met the requirements.

There is no question about what Whitney considered his greatest achievement at Harvard: becoming one of twelve members of his class to join the Porcellian Club, the college's most socially prestigious gathering place. Social position, rather than achievement, was the key to membership, and some of Whitney's student contemporaries, such as Walter Lippmann, the son of prosperous New York Jews, and Joseph Patrick Kennedy, Irish Catholic and Boston Latin School, never would have been considered.

Throughout his Wall Street years, Whitney would display the club's gold pig charm on his vest watch chain. Many years after the fact, FDR would say that his rejection by the club was the greatest disappointment of his life. In John O'Hara's short story "Graven Image," a Porcellian member, seeking a job in Washington from a department undersecretary who was a classmate from a background that would have made club membership impossible, is told, with reference to Whitney's fate: "They tell me a lot of you fellows put them [the gold pig charms] back in your pockets about five years ago, when one of the illustrious brethren closed his downtown office and moved up to Ossining [Sing Sing]". The job seeker replies, "Are you sore at the Pork?"

Whitney left college a tall, well-built, athletic man, with an aloof and somewhat condescending air and obvious self-confidence. Like his older brother George, he was always exquisitely and formally dressed. Aldrich referred to Whitney as "a Tom Buchanan of Wall Street," Buchanan being the polo-playing husband of Daisy in *The Great Gatsby* with "a body capable of enormous leverage—a cruel body." Perhaps another of Fitzgerald's descriptions of Buchanan, this time including Daisy, is more appropriate:

"They were careless people, Tom and Daisy—they smashed up things and creatures…and let other people clean up the mess they had made."

GOMORRAH

We have seen how Harvard, as late as Richard Whitney's time, was still a local institution. Boston, known colloquially as the Hub, was famously self-focused. Remember the story of the Boston dowager who, when asked how she traveled from Boston to California, replied: "Via Dedham."

Old Boston had particularly little use for New York. As Aldrich noted, "Viewed by the old, puritanical, upper classes of New England, this [New York] society seemed something much worse—a dangerously provocative display of vulgar undisciplined wealth that threatened the virtue and stability of the nation."

Perhaps John Adams best caught the Hub's view of its open, diverse, entrepreneurial and—yes—slightly older neighbor: "With all the opulence and splendor of this city [New York], there is very little good breeding to be found. They talk very loud, very fast and all together. If they ask you a question, before you can utter three words of your answer, they will break out upon you again, and talk away."

As the nineteenth century progressed, things only got worse. The Erie Canal—built, owned, and operated by the State of New York—opened in 1825. Suddenly a ton of flour could travel from Buffalo to New York in one-third the time and at one-twelfth the cost. By the 1840s, New York City was handling half the nation's imports and a third of its exports. Ships from 150 countries entered New York harbor each year.

The financial industry—Wall Street—was, relative to today, a smaller part of the whole. Most businesses, even after the Civil War sped change, were local and family-owned. Expansion came through increased earnings. Even such industry titans as Rockefeller, Carnegie, Pratt, and Havemeyer were reluctant to seek outside financing. Their companies resembled many family-controlled corporations found in Europe even today.

The big exception was railroads, where capital needs could be supplied only by outside sources. Between 1830 and 1890, fully half of all American private investment was in railroads. No wonder Henry Clay Frick claimed, "Railroads are the Rembrandts of investment." The vast majority of American securities transactions involved bonds, not stock, and 90 percent were conducted on the New York Stock Exchange. Although the railroad industry eventually overbuilt, it was the nineteenth century's engine of growth, with many other industries reliant on it.

Young men of old money and good education did not flock to Wall Street. James Fenimore Cooper, of old Knickerbocker stock, railed against the "…race of cheating, lying, money-getting blockheads" who did business in lower Manhattan. Senator John C. Calhoun, South Carolina's defender of slavery and the agrarian economy, described Wall Street as a place that looks "…to debts, stocks, banks, distributions, and taxes as the choicest of blessings. The greater the debt—the more abundantly the Stock Market is supplied." Melville, Twain, Whitman, Howells, Wharton, Fitzgerald, and many less renowned writers, decried New York, and particularly Wall Street, and what Henry James called its "appetite at any price." Charles Dickens, on his famous trip to America, compared the city to the infamous biblical city Gomorrah.

As new industrial wealth developed in other cities, its possessors assimilated—often slowly and over generations—into the existing social elites. In New York, where wealth creation was so rapid and marked, this ascension more often resembled a takeover. Nowhere can this be seen more vividly than with the creation of the Metropolitan Opera.

Old New York had its Anglo-Dutch elite, which jealously protected its privileges. New money, dwarfing the old, wanted in. As one commentator put it, "Skirmishes broke out all along the lines of social exclusivity." One battlefront was the Academy of Music, home of the city's grand opera, the most prized of Knickerbocker institutions. Its eighteen boxes were all reserved for the leading old families. When William K. Vanderbilt, the Commodore's grandson, offered an annual contribution of $30,000—an astronomical sum at the time—for one, he was refused.

Rather than bide his time with orchestra seats, Vanderbilt joined Pierpont Morgan, William Rockefeller (John D.'s brother), Jay Gould, George F. Baker, William C. Whitney of subway fame, and others of recent riches, to create a new opera company—the Metropolitan—and build it an opera house. Describing opening night in 1883, one unhappy correspondent wrote, "The Goulds and Vanderbilts and people of that ilk perfumed the air with the odor of crisp greenbacks." Two years later, the Academy of Music closed for good.

Perhaps we should give Frederic de Peyster of the old guard the final word on all this: "Life here has become so exhausting and so expensive that but few of those whose birth or education fit them to adorn any gathering have either the strength or wealth enough to go at the headlong pace of the gilded band of immigrants and natives, the four hundred."

MORGANIZATION

By the turn of the twentieth century, Wall Street could attract men like the Whitney brothers much more readily than during its earlier—and wilder—periods. The prime mover in the Street's transformation was J. Pierpont Morgan and the Morgan bank he created. The story of how he accomplished it begins two generations earlier.

In 1835, George Peabody, a Baltimore dry goods merchant with little formal education, moved to London, then the world's only real financial center. Historian Ron Chernow described him succinctly: "Like many who have overcome early hardship by brute force, he was proud but insecure, always at war with the world and counting his injuries."

Two years later, Peabody opened a merchant banking house, trading in dry goods and financing the trades. Following a common course, the firm moved from merchant to wholesale banking, becoming well known for dealing in American state bonds. Business had its ups and downs, particularly the latter whenever states defaulted—as they did frequently—on their obligations. Between 1841 and 1842, for example, eight states and Florida (then a territory) defaulted.

The ups eventually predominated and Peabody prospered. A bachelor with a reputation for fathering illegitimate and unacknowledged children, contemporaries thought of him as a possible model for Dickens's character Scrooge. In his later years, however, he became a significant philanthropist both in Great Britain and the United States. Museums in several American cities bear his name.

Not in the best of health and approaching sixty, Peabody invited a young American, Junius Spencer Morgan, to come to London and join the firm. The year was 1854. When Peabody retired ten years later, his firm—in effect—became J. S. Morgan and Company (its name until Morgan Grenfell was founded in 1910). Junius's son, J. Pierpont Morgan, would become his father's man in New York, and found J. P. Morgan & Co. Junius would hire another young American, S. Endicott Peabody, a relation of George, whose English-educated son would go on to found the Groton School.

Pierpont Morgan struggled at first in his new city, but then—at age forty-two in 1879—he won a huge commission. By century's end, he had become America's dominant banker and principal architect of a new industrial order.

The deal that made Pierpont's career involved managing the successful sale of 250,000 shares—a substantial minority interest—of New York Central stock bequeathed by Cornelius Vanderbilt to his oldest son, William Henry. The Commodore had left 87 percent of the railroad's equity ownership to William in order to keep the family in control, but two years after the father's death, the son decided to cash in some of his inheritance. Such is the fate of the best of testamentary plans.

The challenge for Pierpont was to liquidate such a large block of stock without causing the share price to drop. The challenge was met, in part, by his ability to find buyers in Great Britain. Pierpont required that he be given a seat on the railroad's board to (in his father's words) "represent the London interests." After accomplishing the Central sale, nothing could hold him back.

Pierpont, as a young man in New York with his English upbringing, may have felt quite superior to his new and often ostentatiously wealthy clients. After all, as Edith Wharton said of the Vanderbilts, "They are entrenched in a sort of Thermopylae of bad taste, from which apparently no force on earth can dislodge them." Morgan built an unpretentious house on Madison Avenue, not the most fashionable location, and his Hudson River country place was relatively modest.

Over time, and perhaps because there was so much money, things got grander. Pierpont's Adirondack camps were more rustic than modest, and *Corsair III*, his last yacht, boasted a waterline length of over

300 feet and a professional crew of seventy. His art collection was valued at $50 million at his death in 1913, while the figure for the rest of the estate was $68.3 million. Everything, of course, is relative. Carnegie, upon learning of the size of Morgan's estate, exclaimed, "And to think he was not a rich man."

The investment banker is stationed between the providers of capital—individuals and institutions—and those needing capital to start, expand, or save their businesses. Increasingly in the years after the Civil War, the banker as underwriter of bonds and (to a lesser extent) stock controlled the territory, with both the issuers of securities and the investors in these securities in dependent roles. Pierpont Morgan played, and perfected, the investment banker's role. There was no need for a sign outside the door at 23 Wall Street. Issuers and investors knew the address. As Chernow put it, "The banker floated high above the workaday world and felt no need to pander to public curiosity."

Morgan, man and bank, has come to symbolize free enterprise, and an economic philosophy based on Adam Smith's invisible hand. In fact, they really represent just the opposite. Pierpont, perhaps reflecting the views of the English aristocracy with whom he identified, found commercial competition unpredictable, wasteful, and just plain vulgar. He valued cooperation over competition and stability over innovation. He became the establishment's banker, and starting with the consolidation of the railroads, moved on to mastermind the creation of the industrial trusts—U. S. Steel, American Smelting and Refining, General Electric, International Harvester, and so many others. Morgan men served on the trust boards. They imposed order and reinforced their own positions at the center of things. Ironically, their political opponents, such as Louis Brandeis, advocate of strict enforcement of the antitrust laws and opponent of large concentrations of economic power, go down in history as adversaries of the marketplace.

As Morganization spread, it turned Wall Street into an increasingly attractive place for ambitious young men of gentlemanly mien to gravitate. Aldrich, commenting on famous polo player Tommy Hitchcock's choice of career, described investment banking as "…in the esteem of his class…the highest occupation next to law." Pierpont made a point of hiring young men of charm and high social position, seemingly without much regard for ability, but also poor men—as often as not without college education—who had obvious talent. Two things contemporaries noticed about his hires were that they were all Protestants and also handsome, in contrast to Pierpont himself.

Robert Bacon provides an example of the first type of Morgan hire. Theodore Roosevelt's Harvard classmate and fellow Porcellian member, Bacon became a Morgan partner in 1894, with the understanding that he would receive 5 percent of the firm's annual profits. Called the Greek god of Wall Street, he had captained the football team at college, rowed on the varsity crew, and distinguished himself as a boxer and track star. Thinking of Robert Bacon, George Wheeler would write, "When the angels of God took unto themselves wives among the daughters of men, the result was the Morgan partners."

After a decade, Bacon left Morgan with lots of money, but also with a reputation as someone with decidedly limited ability. He went on to serve as Theodore Roosevelt's Secretary of State for the final thirty-eight days of TR's administration, and then Ambassador to France under President Taft. In this latter role, he appears to have done Pierpont's bidding in intervening to keep Bessy Marbury, a lover of Pierpont's daughter Anne, from receiving France's Legion of Honor. Pierpont disliked Marbury intensely, blaming her for leading his daughter astray.

In 1916, George Whitney married Bacon's daughter Martha in a grand wedding that included special trains from New York for guests and a reception at the Bacons' country place in Westbury, Long Island. Richard Whitney was his brother's best man, and Endicott Peabody performed the service. Harold Vanderbilt, later of America's Cup and bridge fame, was an usher. George, a rising Morgan executive, would be promoted to partner three years later. His first job after college had been with the Kidder Peabody firm in Boston, Peabody being Endicott's brother. Richard also worked briefly at Kidder before coming to New York.

Examples of the other type of Morgan hire—the poor but able young man—are Harry Davison, son of a plow salesman whose family could not afford to send him to Princeton, and ministers' sons George Perkins and Thomas Lamont. All three of these men served for a time as top Morgan partners, save Pierpont and his son Jack. Historians have noted that hiring practices under Jack and later George Whitney—president from 1940 to 1950 and chairman from 1950 to 1955—favored social background over merit, in contrast to several major competitors.

Morgan served to connect new and old wealth. In a sense, the well-known architect Stanford White did the same with architecture, introducing new money to quality design. Morganization sought to rationalize and control the otherwise unruly business world. It also tried to create and promote a self-defining class of Wall Street men—an elite not unlike the ruling clan that ran the British Empire—who would do the thinking and make the decisions that the business community would follow. To quote Russell Shorto: "The new men of Wall Street, the Morgan men, promised to restore order and rationality to the Street and to the economy over which they presided in a kind of benevolent dictatorship." This was the scene when Richard Whitney left Boston for New York, and thanks to a loan from his Uncle Edward, bought a seat on the New York Stock Exchange. He was twenty-three years old.

GOLCONDA

The decade after his graduation from Harvard was a good one for Richard Whitney. Four years after buying a seat on the New York Stock Exchange, he married Gertrude Sheldon Sands. The widow of a Vanderbilt relation, she was also the daughter of a prominent financial figure who had business connections with Morgan and had served as the finance chairman of the Republican Party and president of the Union League Club. Gertrude's mother, a member of the board of the New York Philharmonic, is credited with recruiting Gustav Mahler to be director. Although Mahler served only two years, he greatly improved the orchestra, but at a personal price. As his somewhat notorious wife Alma noted, "You cannot imagine what Mr. Mahler has suffered. In Vienna, my husband was all-powerful. Even the Emperor did not dictate to him, but in New York he had ten ladies ordering him around like a puppet."

A member of the brokerage firm Cummings & Marckwald, in which his father-in-law had an interest, Whitney renamed the firm Richard Whitney & Company three weeks after his marriage in 1916. While continuing his brokerage business, Richard served during the First World War as a dollar-a-year man on the staff of Herbert Hoover, then the US Food Administrator who became famous for delivering American food supplies to a starving, war-ravaged Europe. Later, President Hoover, concerned with the rapid rise of stock prices in the late 1920s, would invite Whitney to the White House several times for discussions.

In 1919, George Whitney became a Morgan partner, thus securing for the next two decades Richard's position as the principal broker for

Morgan's bond transactions. Year in and out, this Morgan business—amounting to 30 percent of the bank's bond trades—produced $50,000 to $60,000 of annual commission income to Whitney & Company. Based on the Consumer Price Index, $1 in 1929 was worth $12.57 eighty years later.

Secure in their position in the New York financial world as the new decade of the 1920s began, the Whitney brothers must have felt pleased with their good fortune. John Brooks, the renowned business writer, compared Wall Street in the 1920s to Golconda, the legendary Indian city where everyone who passed through became rich. The business center of the country since the opening of the Erie Canal in 1825, New York succeeded London during the First World War as the global financial capital. The war destroyed the financial preeminence of Great Britain, which was forced to abandon the gold standard and run up high, war-related debt. The United States went from the world's largest debtor nation before the war to the largest creditor nation by war's end. How things change.

Ill-prepared as it was to take the lead on the world stage, the Street's confidence in itself never flagged. The financial community's high self-regard was on full display in its reaction to the events of September 16, 1920, when a horse-drawn wagon turned the corner in front of the Morgan headquarters at 23 Wall Street just before noon and exploded in a tremendous and—for some—fatal blast. The scars from the explosion, some an inch deep, can still be seen on the north facade of the unnamed, low-rise Morgan building, then Morgan's headquarters, reflecting in their continued visibility the confidence and defiance of the bank's management. As the smoke billowed through the building immediately after the blast, a French visitor asked several Morgan partners with whom he was meeting, "Does this thing happen often?" The next day it was business as usual. The crime remains unsolved.

The Whitneys' association with Morgan was particularly felicitous. From the 1880s through the 1920s, Morgan was the dominant Wall Street institution. During the financial panic of 1907, Pierpont Morgan locked his fellow bankers in his library until they agreed to support a market bailout, in effect acting as a private central bank. In 1913, a real central bank—the Federal Reserve System—was created, perhaps beginning the gradual decline in Morgan influence. That same year,

Pierpont died and was succeeded by his son Jack, who remained ever the English gentleman and ardent Episcopalian (albeit with a touch of the family's earlier Puritanism—for example, bank executives were not permitted to divorce). Class-conscious and self-righteous, without his father's self-confidence and aggressiveness, Jack had an obvious ambivalence toward trade, particularly the buying and selling on the Stock Exchange. He never entered the Exchange, knew nothing of its operations, and preferred to have the bank trade through independent brokers, of whom Richard Whitney was the most prominent.

If Morgan had a rival, it was Kuhn, Loeb & Co., particularly after it became the financial ally of E. H. Harriman in his railroad creations and consolidations. Rockefeller also preferred Kuhn Loeb, finding Pierpont Morgan "...very haughty, very much inclined to look down on other men...I have never been able to see why any man should have such a high and mighty feeling about himself." Kuhn Loeb, under Jacob Schiff and then Otto Kahn, the latter being perhaps the greatest patron of the arts in American history, operated much like Morgan—no advertising, no overt solicitation, no price competition, no direct stealing of others' clients. How surprised Pierpont Morgan and Jacob Schiff would be to see the huge electric sign—complete with brightly illuminated stock ticker—marking Morgan Stanley's current headquarters above Times Square.

Morgan was Protestant, an Anglophile, sporting, and a conduit for British investment in the United States, with its partners representing its investors on corporate boards. Kuhn Loeb was German, Jewish, supportive of the arts, and a conduit for continental European investment in America. Particularly during the First World War, there was considerable tension between the Yankee and Jewish Wall Street worlds, and countless examples of the former's anti-Semitism. According to Chernow, Richard Whitney was known for "blackballing" Jews from the high echelons of the Exchange's governance. George Whitney wrote Jack Morgan in 1936 complaining about the "Jewish lawyer element" behind the Senate investigation of Wall Street. During the 1920s, a few Irish Catholics began to appear—Joe Kennedy, Michael Meehan, and "Sell'em Ben" Smith—often at the far edges of respectability.

Unrecognized by most observers at the time, including Richard Whitney, things were changing on Wall Street and in the world financial community during the 1920s. The decade saw the beginnings of a subtle decline in power and importance of the investment banks acting as the indispensable middlemen between the providers and the users of capital. The providers—investment trusts, mutual funds, retail investors, endowments, eventually pension funds—became more and more powerful. The users grew into giants able to raise money with less dependence on investment banks. At the New York Stock Exchange, power was flowing gradually away from the old guard of floor traders and specialists, with their advocacy of fixed commissions and governance rules of their own devising, and toward the so-called commission brokers whose customer base was the general public. The commission brokers understood that the Exchange could only succeed if seen by the public as fair and transparent.

Hidden by the surface glare of the decade's prosperity, seeds were being sown that would culminate in the Depression. Depressed farm prices and the Florida mid-decade land bust were warning signs of what was coming. As already noted, Great Britain abandoned the gold standard in 1916. By the time it resumed gold payments in 1925, at the pre-war exchange rate of 113 grams of gold per pound sterling, it was much too late to sustain the old exchange rate. As the dollar also had a fixed peg (23.22 grams), any rise in its relative attractiveness would cause gold to flow to the United States.

Benjamin Strong Jr., president of the Federal Reserve Bank of New York and America's key central banker—a great Anglophile and close friend of his British counterpart—kept US interest rates low through 1927 in order to support the pound. As Liaquat Ahamed pointed out in *Lords of Finance: The Bankers Who Broke the World*, holding US interest rates down contributed substantially to the stock bubble and subsequent crash at decade's end. Winston Churchill, who was Chancellor of the Exchequer in 1925, later said that returning the United Kingdom to the gold standard was the greatest mistake he ever made.

THE JAZZ AGE

When the First World War ended in 1919, Richard Whitney was thirty years old. To be a bond broker in an era of fixed commissions, secure in representing the financial community's most prestigious institution, was lucrative and easy. Known as "the Morgan broker" and "the voice of Morgan," the latter to the displeasure of some actual Morgan partners, Whitney took home slightly more than half his firm's profits. His four to six partners, none of whom had a financial investment in the firm, shared the remains. In fact, it was never clear just who was a partner and what it meant to be one. One was a fellow Porcellian alumnus, but another essentially a clerk whose name appeared on partner lists. A Morgan partner once referred to Whitney's partners as office boys.

For sure, Richard Whitney & Company was a one-man show. Whitney testified in 1938 that he always considered the firm as his alone. He never bothered to call a partners' meeting, and kept key information about the business to himself. He maintained a "control account" known only to his accountant and personal secretary. In the words of Harold Mehling, "He [Whitney] ignored them [his partners] in the same way he ignored as much of the world as he could."

Although the Liberty Bond campaign during the First World War succeeded in attracting middle-class investors, and stock ownership broadened in the 1920s (partly through mutual funds and bank-created trusts), securities investing—that is, bonds and stocks—remained mostly a game for wealthier individuals and established institutions. A broker's success depended more on social connections than on financial acumen or hard work. Whitney had these connections, albeit initially through his school ties, wife, and brother, rather than through family wealth. As Noah Feldman has noted, "Money certainly granted entrée into governing circles, but education was probably more important to the way the Protestant elite defined itself."

According to testimony he gave before Congress in the early 1930s, Whitney took home about $60,000 annually from the firm, or about $800,000 to $900,000 in today's dollars. The Morgan business represented about half of firm revenues, while retail brokerage on behalf of a few social friends and Far Hills neighbors produced the rest. The top marginal federal tax rate during the 1920s was 24 percent—it would go to 70 percent by 1936—but there were ways of protecting much of one's income. Whitney once told a would-be creditor that his wife's holdings were worth $500,000.

Had he been so inclined, Whitney could have built his firm into a powerhouse. The tectonic plates under Wall Street were shifting in the 1920s—albeit gradually—toward retail customers and professional investors, as well as toward the giant corporate borrowers that were becoming more independent of their investment bankers. Of course, even if Whitney had anticipated the coming changes, he would have needed great drive and energy to take advantage of the situation. One senses with him, however, about the same level of enthusiasm for the brokerage business as evidenced by Nick Carraway, the narrator in *The Great Gatsby*. Nick, conscious that he had many rich classmates, became a bond broker after graduating from Yale: "Everyone I know went to Wall Street in the 1920s, so I supposed it could support one more single man. All my aunts and uncles talked it over as if they were choosing a prep school for me, and finally said 'Why—yes.'" Whitney may have been a little embarrassed—or disappointed—at being just a broker. The most prestigious jobs on Wall Street were those of the investment bankers. Think of Richard's contemporaries such as Tom Lamont, Russell Leffingwell, Dwight Morrow, Herbert Lehman. Robert Lovett, the Harriman brothers, and—of course—George Whitney. Corporate lawyers, such as John McCloy, Henry Stimson, the Dulles brothers, John W. Davis, even—briefly—FDR, also enjoyed great prestige.

While Whitney may have found brokerage a bit dull or tawdry, he did find another outlet for his business passions: venture capital. Very early in his career, he became deeply involved in investing in start-up companies created to do such things as convert peat humus into commercial fertilizer or mine mineral colloids. As commentator Ormonde de Kay has noted: "Behind his beautifully tailored exterior...there lurked...a very different individual: a gambler who much preferred taking fliers in speculative stocks to the profitable but humdrum business of dealing in bonds." As we will see, Whitney early on—starting in 1926 with his wife's family money—pledged securities held by him for his clients as security for bank loans.

Bad investments were only part of the problem. The other road to his eventual ruin was a lifestyle he couldn't afford. His modus operandi—like Uncle Edward's and brother George's—was not the quiet, old-money style. First there was the estate in the horse country around Far Hills, New Jersey, which he bought, reputedly with his wife's money, while still in his twenties. Originally 231 acres, the place grew through subsequent purchases to 495 acres—more than double its original size. Elected to the Bedminster Township governing committee at age thirty-one, he represented the fox-hunting fraternity's interest in keeping the local roads unpaved, and thus easily passable by horse and rider. Whitney became master, or president, of the Essex Fox Hounds, and rode to the hounds on one of twenty horses he owned. As master, he was expected to lead the field of other riders, with the professional huntsman and whips controlling the hounds.

In town, Whitney bought a five-story, Georgian-style house, which still stands at 115 East Seventy-third Street. His club affiliations in New York included the Links, where he was president at the time of his fall in 1938. His faded photograph can still be seen hanging on presidents' row on the club's first floor. He was treasurer of the New York Yacht Club and a member of the Racquet and Tennis, Knickerbocker, Harvard, Turf and Field, and Jockey clubs. In Boston, he belonged to the Somerset and Racquet clubs, and in New Jersey, to the Somerset Hills Country Club, Essex Fox Hounds, and the Lake Club. He served on the executive committee of the National Steeplechase and Hunt Association, fox hunting's governing board.

Endicott Peabody urged his Groton boys to contribute to society. Whitney did not seem to feel much noblesse oblige, as was noted before his criminal sentencing in the probation officer's report. Other than occasionally participating in fundraising efforts for the Salvation Army or a Manhattan settlement house or the like, or serving on the township committee in New Jersey, his voluntary commitments mostly involved social and sporting clubs and activities.

In trying to understand what motivated Whitney, some commentators have wondered whether he might have felt sibling rivalry with his older and successful brother. Certainly George was a hard act to follow, although follow Richard did, from Groton to Harvard, to Porcellian, to New York and Wall Street and a Morgan relationship, to marriage to a successful financier's daughter, to country estates and East Side townhouses, to membership in virtually every club in town. Richard made the cover of *Time* in 1934 as president of the New York Stock Exchange and enemy of the New Deal financial reforms, and his obituary was longer than his brother's. Nevertheless, George remained the more successful brother.

Contemporaries saw George as the quieter and more intellectual of the two brothers. The year he became a Morgan partner, in 1919, he accompanied senior partner Tom Lamont to the Paris Peace Conference ending the First World War, the latter being a member of the American delegation. During the 1920s, it became increasingly obvious that George was being groomed to succeed Lamont as the de facto head of Morgan. In the early 1930s, he accompanied Jack Morgan, Lamont, and other Morgan partners to various congressional hearings on reforming Wall Street, and the older men often referred technical questions to him. After passage of the Glass-Steagall Act in 1933, George was deeply involved with splitting Morgan into a commercial bank (J. P. Morgan & Co.) and an investment bank (Morgan Stanley). In 1940, he became the first president of the commercial bank in its corporate—as opposed to partnership—form, and later became chairman of the board.

In terms of business importance, it is interesting to compare corporate directorships. Richard was a director of the Corn Exchange Bank, a relatively modest bank from which, as we shall see later, he borrowed $500,000. George, as was the Morgan custom, was on the boards of many of the bank's clients. In 1933 alone, he served on eighteen corporate boards, including those of General Motors, Johns Manville, Kennecott Copper, Montgomery Ward, New York Central,

Pullman, Texas Gulf Sulphur, and Guarantee Trust. His foundation boards included Markle and Sloan.

As for lifestyle, George more than kept up with Richard. In the late 1920s, he built a grand Georgian townhouse at 120 East Eightieth Street, with Clarence Dillon and John Jacob Astor as neighbors. He owned a yacht 108 feet in length, and was a leading Westbury country squire. His country house, designed by Delano & Aldrich, was built on Bacon family land. He served as president of the Harvard Club of New York and the Harvard Board of Overseers, and later received an honorary degree from the university. Richard did have his own Harvard connection—the advisory committee to the Department of Economics—from which he resigned when he went to prison. While president of the Exchange, he received an honorary degree from the School of Commerce at New York University.

LEADER

On Wednesday, October 23, 1929, Richard Whitney was little known outside the fox-hunting circles and fashionable clubs. His brokerage business was steady, but not growing. He seemed to find it boring. The transformation of the private man into a public figure began the next day—Black Thursday—with his dramatic buying stroll on the floor of the Exchange.

The gambit appeared to work. When the ticker tape finally fell silent, more than four hours after closing, the day's volume—over 13 million shares traded—was three times the previous record. Share prices, however, were only moderately off for the day. It had been a remarkable afternoon turnaround. In Friday's papers, Senator Wilson, Republican from Indiana, was quoted as blaming Black Thursday on the Democratic Party's opposition to high tariffs. The New York Times editorialized that the financial community was now "secure in the knowledge that the most powerful banks in the country stood ready to prevent a recurrence [of panic]."

Of course, we now know success was short-lived. On Monday, the bankers behind the Black Thursday rescue reconvened. They had lost their will, however, and adjourned without agreeing on any joint action. The next day, October 29, was the worst day in New York Stock Exchange history. By late 1932, stock prices would be down 89 percent from their 1929 highs. Even in nominal dollars and despite significant inflation, these highs would not be reached again until 1954.

Whitney called a meeting of the governing committee for noon on the twenty-ninth. To keep things secret, it was held in a small office directly below the trading floor. Here is Whitney's description of the meeting:

> *The office they met in was never designed for large meetings of this sort, with the result that most of the Governors were compelled to stand, or to sit on tables. As the meeting proceeded, panic was raging overhead on the floor. Every few minutes the latest prices were announced, with quotations moving swiftly and irresistibly downwards. The feeling of those present was revealed by their habit of continually lighting cigarettes, taking a puff or two, putting them out and lighting new ones—a practice which soon made the narrow room blue with smoke and extremely stuffy.*

Literally overnight, from his stock buying stroll on Black Thursday to the next morning's headlines, Richard Whitney became a national figure. In the ensuing few weeks—the actual president of the Exchange did not return from his honeymoon until December—Whitney, as acting president, performed magnificently. He fought to keep the Exchange open, fearing that to do otherwise would be seen as weakness. He offered the outside world a calm and confident presence. He encouraged everyone to "get your smiles on, boys" and be positive. The press described him as more an aristocrat than a market man, part of and yet above the seething hubbub: "the highest type of Wall Street broker."

Whitney took to his new role, difficult as times were. He had a sense for the dramatic, such as keeping the stock tickers going while he spoke from the Exchange's rostrum to the trading floor below. Always the fox hunter, he later said that during debate over closure, "The authorities of the Exchange led the life of hunted things, until [eventually] the desirability of holding the market open became apparent to all." Brooks said of Whitney:

> *But one may believe that part of him loved it; to command, to be thus relied on, to have the moral authority of a Groton prefect combined with the naked power of a potential temporal messiah is heady stuff, and Whitney had so superbly the patrician bearing, the aloof air, the broad shoulders, the steady gaze, the ready smile to carry off the role.*

At the end of November, the Exchange's governing committee passed a resolution thanking Whitney for his leadership: "Great emergencies produce the men who are competent to deal with them." Several months later Stock Exchange Post No. 2, where Whitney made his first Black Thursday purchase—"205 for Steel"—was presented to him. It remained on display in the lobby of his firm's office until his fall, when it was sold in bankruptcy for five dollars.

Hardest hit by the events of late October 1929 were those who bought some shares, usually about half the total purchase, outright, and the rest "on margin" provided by lenders—banks and other corporations attracted by high interest rates. The shares bought outright were pledged as collateral for the margin loans that produced the cash to buy the additional shares. When the price of the pledged shares dropped, the lender demanded additional cash immediately to protect the loan. When additional cash was not forthcoming, the pledged shares were sold.

As we learned only too well in recent years, leverage is a two-edged sword, wonderful on the upswing and destructive in decline. If a buyer buys stock on margin and the price of the shares goes up, the buyer gets the full benefit, as the loan stays the same. He also may receive dividends based on the total number of shares. He will have to pay interest on the margin loan—8 to 15 percent in the late 1920s—but this is a small price to pay if share prices are rising.

Margin lending for stock purchase had grown dramatically through the 1920s, from maybe $1 billion in the early years of the decade to $3.5 billion in 1927, and almost $6 billion in 1928. By the end of the decade, it is estimated that about six hundred thousand individuals and families were buying on margin, out of a total population of 1.5 million stock investors. These numbers may not seem large in comparison with the total US population of the time—120 million—but, as economist John Kenneth Galbraith pointed out, "The striking thing about the stock market speculation of 1929 was not the massiveness of the participation. Rather it was the way it became central in the culture."

Until the 1929 crash, Whitney had done little to distinguish himself on the Street. He had, however, served since 1919 as one of forty-plus governors of the Exchange, and on many of its committees. With his

Morgan and social connections, he was a safe and natural choice for advancement, becoming vice president in 1928. The board was controlled by specialists and floor brokers, and was considered by all involved to be a kind of comfortable club. The governors and board officers served gratis, while employed full time at member firms, and little was required of them. The Exchange was entirely self-regulated, which meant it was essentially unregulated.

With the crash, Whitney had become the Exchange's human form, its symbol and spokesman. The papers covered his comings and goings. In April 1930, during a market rally from its late 1929 lows, he was elected to the first of five consecutive annual terms as Exchange president. His election was well received as someone who, despite his haughty and superior style, would be a good spokesman. Again, as Brooks put it:

> ...he flourished in a time when many Americans still actually preferred to be influenced and led by those they felt to be socially above them. His very aloofness and unwillingness to stoop to or compromise with public taste served to impress the public; it might not love him—few did—but it listened to him and believed him.

THE VOICE OF WALL STREET

Immediately after being elected president of the Exchange in April 1930—at age forty-one, the youngest ever—Whitney embarked on a national speaking tour that took him to many major cities over the next five years. His typical audience was the local chamber of commerce, but sometimes his speeches were broadcast nationally on radio and covered in film clips that supplemented feature movies in the era before television news. By the time he appeared on the cover of *Time* in February 1934, portrayed as the defender of Wall Street against New Deal reforms, he was already well known in this role. Although some found him too remote and superior in personal style, one can't help but wonder—as people did at the time—whether Whitney might not have gravitated toward the political arena had events developed differently. In 1940, the Republicans nominated Wendell Willkie, a utilities company executive who had fought the creation of the Tennessee Valley Authority, as its candidate to oppose FDR's third term.

A dozen or so of Whitney's speeches are carefully preserved in the archives of the Exchange. Apparently the result of a joint effort by the Exchange's communications department, its in-house economist, and Whitney, the speeches draw conclusions, but offer little analysis. Whitney may have been the landed English aristocrat in private life, albeit the New Jersey variety, but in public he was a market man. In his view, the Exchange was "a perfect institution," free markets self-corrected, and regulation led to socialism. John Maynard Keynes once wrote: "Practical men, who believe themselves to be quite exempt from any intellectual influences, are usually the slaves of some defunct economist." A *New York Times* editorial in 1932 described Whitney's views as "inexorable."

For Whitney, the first order of business in his public appearances was to deflect blame for the growing economic collapse away from the stock market. While he admitted that, along with almost everyone else, he hadn't seen the crash coming, he was absolutely sure, as he was about so much, that the Stock Exchange was not to blame. "To attribute business depressions to stock-market panics is to place the cart before the horse." He blamed the "business slump" on overproduction and artificially high prices. He saw the stock market as a "barometer" of the underlying economy. Whitney later noted that the market crash had cost him $2 million, presumably in paper losses.

It is true that the Federal Reserve index of industrial production stood at 117 in October 1929, down from 126 in June. In fact, several other economic indices declined as the year progressed.

For example, steel production had been off since June; homebuilding was off all year and had been for several years running; freight-car loadings were off starting in October. Whatever the immediate pre-crash decline, however, it was modest, and not unlike previous declines earlier in the decade. Longer-term problems, such as the inability of farmers to raise prices during the 1920s and the post-1926 Florida land bust, seem largely unrelated to stock-market performance.

That lax money-lending practices had led to a stock bubble that led directly to the market crash was a possibility Whitney found difficult to confront. His infallible Exchange, by allowing margin purchases with virtually no restrictions, had revealed its fallibility. Even after the crash, the Exchange did little to restrict buying on margin. This unwillingness on the part of the Exchange to police itself was highly upsetting to President Herbert Hoover. While Whitney's clients didn't buy on margin, several ran large deficits on their accounts.

What external forces drove stock speculation? With the United Kingdom unable to support the pound at the pre-First World War value of $4.86 an ounce, gold flowed to the United States. The Federal Reserve cut the discount rate to as low as 3.5 percent, which hardly seems low by recent standards, and purchased government securities in order to inflate the money supply. In doing so, Benjamin Strong of the

New York Fed hoped to weaken the attraction of the United States as an investment location, and thus halt the gold flow across the Atlantic.

It didn't work. What it did achieve was a stock market bubble, with margin loans and easy money driving prices up. The great rise in share prices began in 1927, but took off in 1928, the year the New York Times industrial average went from 245 to 331. The huge increases mostly involved the shares of a few major companies: RCA went from 85 to 420; Montgomery Ward from 117 to 440; and DuPont from 310 to 525. By the time Strong's successor—worried about excessive borrowing—moved to raise the discount rate in early 1929, it was too late to pierce the bubble. Despite his membership on the New York Federal Reserve Board, Charles E. Mitchell, "Sunshine Charlie," who ran National City Bank and promoted stock purchases through the bank's national securities affiliates, openly defied the Fed's attempt to rein in borrowing. Mitchell declared: "We feel we have an obligation which is paramount to any Federal Reserve warning [to keep on fueling buying on margin]." Of course, National City was happy to borrow from the Fed at 5 percent, and lend these borrowed funds to margin speculators at something like 12 percent. In his Memoirs, Hoover would call Benjamin Strong "a mental annex to Europe" and accuse him of "crimes far worse than murder." One wonders what President Obama must think of Alan Greenspan.

Who did predict the crash? Certainly not President Calvin Coolidge, who, a few days before he was succeeded by Herbert Hoover in March 1929, pronounced stocks "cheap at current prices." Not Andrew W. Mellon, Secretary of the Treasury under three presidents, whom Galbraith described as a passionate advocate of inaction. Hoover, ironically, given the way history has treated him, was ahead of almost everyone in seeing the potential for trouble as stock prices rose.

Predictably, others later claimed clairvoyance, but may have been as lucky as they were smart. Bernard Baruch, often credited with selling securities slightly before the collapse, also said in June 1929, "The economic condition of the world seems on the verge of a great forward movement." On September 5, 1928, Roger Babson, a gadfly educator and prognosticator, predicted that "[s]ooner or later a crash is coming, and it may be terrific." In September 1928, however, he also had predicted that "[t]he election of Hoover and a Republican congress should result in continued prosperity for 1929."

No group was as blind as the top academics. Professor Joseph Stagg Lawrence of Princeton, in a book published in 1929, wrote: "The consensus of judgment of the millions whose valuations function on that admirable market, the Stock Exchange, is that stocks are not at present overvalued. Where is that group of men with the all-embracing wisdom which will entitle them to veto the judgment of this intelligent multitude?"

Graduates of other universities shouldn't feel too smug. Yale's Professor Irving Fisher, just before the crash, opined: "Stock prices have reached what looks like a permanently high plateau." Meanwhile, up in Cambridge, a group of Harvard economists—the Harvard Economic Society—stated in November 1929: "A severe depression like that of 1920-21 is outside the range of probability. We are not facing protracted liquidation." Galbraith noted that the Society reiterated this position until it itself was liquidated.

In his public presentations, Whitney never tried to deny that times were tough, and getting tougher. "There have been…too many empty platitudes, too great a lack of frankness and realism, too much an attitude of trying to whistle in the graveyard at midnight." And yet, in part by his mere presence, he always conveyed a sense that things would get better "in this marvelous country of ours."

With an air of great candor, Whitney also recognized the presence of dishonest men in the securities industry. He admitted that investors were sometimes bilked for large sums. The Exchange was, however, doing everything that could be done to expose wrongdoers. "The fraudulent security criminal is a coward." To combat such bad actors, Whitney asserted that "[w]e [the Stock Exchange] endeavor to have righteous men as our members and to have their business done in a straightforward way." At the time he made these statements, no one would have recognized the irony.

THE NATIONAL STAGE

During the first month of his presidency in 1929, Herbert Hoover invited Richard Whitney to the White House. Whitney was only the Exchange's vice president at the time, but the two men knew each other from their days at the United States Food Administration during the First World War. Hoover, concerned about a stock-price bubble, urged Whitney to get the Exchange to take actions to dampen speculation. Whitney promised he would do so, but in fact did nothing. A second White House meeting, this time for dinner, took place in October 1930, and was described as "a delightful meeting" by the Exchange's new vice president, who also attended. Again, promises of self-regulation were made, but went largely unfulfilled.

While the stock market rallied for a time in 1930, that year also saw the passage of the wrongheaded Smoot-Hawley tariffs. In July 1931, the United Kingdom abandoned the gold standard for the second and final time. US industrial production kept falling. By the end of the next year—1932—the stock market had declined 89 percent from its 1929 high, and the US unemployment rate had reached 25 percent. With breadlines all over the country, people were desperate.

Washington seemed either to freeze or make the wrong moves. Hoover, the humanitarian Quaker engineer, was constrained by his pro-market, small-government philosophy. Concerning the Exchange, he advocated reforms such as restrictions on margin lending and short selling. At least until his final year in office, however, he believed these reforms should be the result of self-regulation by the Exchange, rather than of government imposition. This was fine with Whitney, who once noted with pride, "No public agency…exercises any regulatory power over [the Stock Exchange]."

By 1932, Hoover's views were changing, as was evident at a third White House meeting with Whitney in January of that year. In his *Memoirs*, Hoover wrote that he "warned Richard Whitney…that unless they took measures to clean their own house, he would ask Congress to investigate the Stock Exchange with a view to Federal control legislation." What happened? As Hoover later wrote, "Mr. Whitney made profuse promises, but did nothing."

Perhaps Hoover's frustration was magnified by his steadily declining chances for reelection, in November 1932, to a second term. He needed a scapegoat to deflect criticism of his own performance, or lack thereof. He also was concerned about persistent rumors—absolutely unsubstantiated—that leading Democrats with Wall Street connections were organizing raids that would—through short selling—drive stock prices even lower, thus damaging his reelection chances. He told reporters that short sellers were bringing "discouragement to the country as a whole."

In February, Hoover publicly called for the Senate Committee on Banking and Currency to investigate the financial industry, despite Tom Lamont's plea not to do so. Hoover may still have had reservations about federal regulation, but an investigation, at the least, might force the Exchange to do more to regulate itself. The major focus would be on pools and short selling, where the seller has a vested interest in falling share prices. Hoover made it clear that his first choice would be for the Exchange itself "to take adequate measures to protect investors from artificial depression of the price of securities from speculative profit."

The Democrats had taken control of the House of Representatives in 1930, but the Senate remained Republican until the 1932 elections. The chairman of the Senate's banking committee was Peter Norbeck, a progressive South Dakota Republican, pro-farm and anti-Wall Street, who, with little formal education, had made his fortune drilling artesian farm wells. He had no pretense about understanding the securities and banking industries. He said of himself, "As an authority on banking and currency he was the ablest well-driller in Congress." As the financial crisis deepened, he said, "I really begin to think I am fortunate in the fact that part of the stuff goes over my head—I do not understand it all. If I did, maybe I wouldn't sleep."

If Norbeck was ill-prepared, so were most of the other committee members and staff. On Friday afternoon, April 8, 1932, Richard Whitney was subpoenaed at his house in New York and ordered to appear on Monday in Washington as the committee's first witness. He would testify for nine days and, at least in the early going, win the battle for public opinion. In fact, he made the Senate look foolish.

It was standing room only in the Senate hearing room, with some spectators sitting on filing boxes. The national press was there. The senators' ignorance was obvious. One confused Richard with his brother, George. Whitney, in high Brahmin style, lectured and corrected with what Brooks called "weary patrician tolerance." There was no need for the federal government to act; the Exchange was successful at policing itself; raids to depress shares were forbidden by Exchange rules—indirectly—as actions that "demoralize the market." Whitney was emphatic when he testified that a raid "driving down a stock's price is a violation of the rules of the New York Stock Exchange. And it does not take place."

Of course, throughout the 1920s, raids took place all the time. In 1929 alone, over one hundred stocks on the Exchange were "put in play" in pool schemes. Typically, a number of traders, operating under the instructions of a pool manager such as Michael Meehan and "Sell'em Ben" Smith, would buy a given company's stock at ever-increasing prices. Often, business reporters were paid to promote the shares. Companies with glamour appeal and relatively small numbers of outstanding shares were particular targets. When the share price had risen to the desired level, the pool manager would "pull the plug" and start selling. Pool participants bought shares short, borrowing shares with the idea that they would pay back their debts with cheaper shares after the share price had collapsed. In reality, the stock pool was a way for the ticker tape to tell a false story. It is said that the tape doesn't lie, but it certainly can be manipulated.

In his testimony during the first nine days of the committee's hearing, Whitney was adamant about the necessary role short selling plays in the market, and about how disastrous it would be to outlaw the practice. He argued that short selling was simply the sale of something at a given price for future delivery. Every short sale assumes a later purchase by the short seller to cover the initial sale. The problem with Whitney's argument, however, was that it created and focused on the straw man of absolute prohibition. As securities lawyer William R. Perkins's widely circulated rebuttal made clear at the time, the issue wasn't absolute prohibition but reasonable regulation to protect the innocent investor. In his testimony and speeches on the subject, Whitney essentially equated regulation with prohibition, making reasonable discussion virtually impossible. Whitney did support a brief halt in short sales by the Exchange after the British announced their second abandonment of the gold standard.

What Whitney refused to recognize was that short selling had become an integral part of stock manipulation in the years leading up to the crash. Even compared with his Wall Street brothers, his was a hard line. Otto Kahn of Kuhn Loeb had no trouble telling the Senate committee that pooling was an "artificial, antisocial, illegitimate practice which thrives on the gullibility of the public."

Reading the transcripts of the Senate committee hearing, one can sense the rising frustration of the senators and staff as Whitney refused to concede that there was any problem with the Exchange itself, or the practices of margin buying, short selling, and pool manipulation. Senator Brookhart of Iowa charged: "You brought this country to the greatest panic in history." Whitney replied: "We have brought this country, sir, to its standing in the world through speculation."

The obvious fact was that the senators had neither the knowledge nor the staff to compete with Whitney. For example, Norbeck confronted Whitney, saying, "You make rules that are just paper rules." Whitney asked for proof, to which Norbeck could only reply: "You attend these hearings for a while and we will give you some proof." Whitney's reply: "I have." The *Wall Street Journal*, predictable even then, complained of the committee's "abuse of inquisitorial power." One cartoon portrayed Whitney as a teacher and the senators as schoolboys.

On April 21, Whitney's ninth day of testimony, Senator Norbeck exclaimed, "You don't grant that anything in the market is illegal. You don't grant anything. You're hopeless." He then dismissed Whitney, saying, "Oh, you will be back." Another committee member described Whitney as the most arrogant and uncooperative witness he had ever encountered. And yet, as reflected in the news stories at the time, the victory remained Whitney's.

With the fall elections approaching, the committee adjourned in June. Norbeck's honest evaluation of the job it had done so far: "The committee had spent a great deal of time trying to prove up on short selling as having a far-reaching effect on the market. Our best effort did not result in anything substantial, though everyone knows that."

The November 1932 elections changed everything. Franklin Roosevelt easily wrested the presidency from Hoover, and the Democrats took control of the Senate. Although Norbeck—who refused to endorse his fellow Republican Hoover and would support FDR publicly in 1936—bucked the Democratic tide to win reelection, he knew he would lose his committee chairmanship—and the chance to achieve something of lasting importance—on Inauguration Day, March 4, 1933. He recognized the potential of his committee's work. "This is the greatest opportunity I have had for broad work since I came to Washington," he said.

In the time he had remaining, Norbeck was determined to reinvigorate his committee's stalled investigation. After a few false starts, he hired a former chief assistant district attorney of Manhattan— Sicilian-born, a cobbler's son, and a Tammany Democrat—as counsel. His name was Ferdinand Pecora, a man whose background and prosecutorial style were in obvious contrast to Whitney's and those of other witnesses from Wall Street. It would prove to be a fateful choice.

With only six weeks before Inauguration Day, Pecora decided to focus on "the issue and distribution of securities," and among others, issued subpoenas to Charles E. Mitchell, chairman of National City Bank, and two fellow executives. The bank's investment affiliates, operating nationally, were the largest sellers of securities during the late 1920s. Chase and a few other large banks had similar operations.

Sunshine Charlie Mitchell, the greatest securities salesman of his era and a director of fifty-nine corporations, appeared before the committee on February 21, only ten days before Inauguration Day. In the ensuing few days, Mitchell and his associates would become utterly disgraced for having awarded excessive compensation to themselves, and peddling shoddy securities to unsuspecting customers. The hearings laid the groundwork for the Banking Act of 1933—Glass-Steagall—

prohibiting investment banks from accepting deposits and requiring nationally chartered banks to sever their securities-selling affiliates. The law also created the Federal Deposit Insurance Corporation.

On the ninth day of hearings, Thursday, March 2, only two days before Norbeck would lose control of the committee, Whitney was called back, almost a year after his earlier appearance. The day before, Whitney had given a curious speech in Cleveland in which he seemed to criticize Mitchell without mentioning his name. He talked about "ephemeral profits" of the "boom years." Despite this, he explicitly exempted the Exchange from any failure to protect investors. Rather, according to Whitney, it was the investors themselves who gave their "confidence too readily" to people they wrongly considered "business or financial geniuses." He blamed the public for investing in securities offerings "without inquiry into his [the presenter's] qualifications and training and without much thought of the soundness of his enterprise." Was Whitney softening toward regulation?

Under questioning, the answer to this became clear. Whitney was not softening much. Pecora asked him whether the Exchange ever audited the companies that sought to be listed. He answered, "No," but it had recently required newly listed companies to have an independent audit. Did the Exchange review the "character" of the top executives or directors of listed companies? Only at the initial listing, answered Whitney. The Exchange had the power to delist a company, but this almost never happened. As Pecora set out the limits of Exchange enforcement practices, Whitney replied that no form of regulation—by the Exchange or the government—could stop outright fraud. "Mr. Pecora," he said, "naturally if people want to be crooked and to make false statements, they may get away with it with any agency or institution."

Pecora replied, "In other words, the Exchange proceeds upon the assumption that nobody lies to it, does it?"

"The Exchange," Whitney countered, "has got to take people at their face value and that they are honest until they are proven otherwise." He saw no need to operate under "the presumption of dishonesty" and to doubt the integrity of those whose companies were listed.

"In other words, you would rather discover the dishonesty after it has come to light or after its evil effects have been manifested, than prevent the dishonesty beforehand?"

"But that has not happened, Mr. Pecora."

"How do you know it has not happened?"

Whitney kept insisting that the Exchange existed "to allow the ready action of the law of supply and demand." Pecora asked whether the free market wasn't undercut by the ability of pools "to exercise temporarily...a control of the market price?" Whitney admitted this could happen. "Now," Pecora asked, "what steps, if any, does the Exchange take to prevent that kind of control?" Answer: "I do not know of any, Mr. Pecora."

Still, Whitney continued to assert that pools didn't undercut the goal of free and open markets. Pecora asked, "When such a pool is operating and affecting such a control, it is restricting a free open market where honest values can be obtained, is it not?" Whitney replied, "No, sir." Pecora once more asked, "Is it not?" Whitney again answered, "No, sir."

In Pecora's view, the Exchange "was in reality neither more or less than a glorified gambling casino where the odds were heavily weighted against the eager outsiders." He saw the public as victims of insiders manipulating the system. The ten days of hearings had shown he largely was right.

This time, Whitney did not win the public to his side. He was testy and defensive. One commentator noted his "self-importance and righteous attitude." It was clear that the Exchange had done too little to combat the manipulation by insiders at the expense of the general investors. As Benjamin Cohen, a New Deal lawyer, put it, after Pecora "Congress was ready to pass anything" to correct securities trading and banking abuses. After the 2008 financial debacle, Ron Chernow wrote an opinion piece for The New York Times titled: "Where Is Our Ferdinand Pecora?"

Whitney and the Exchange's old guard could live— unhappily— with the increased disclosure required by the 1933 Securities Act. The 1934 Act creating the Securities and Exchange Commission was another matter. Whitney claimed the act would "destroy the free and open market for securities" and turn lower Manhattan into "a deserted village." It was true, as Will Rogers put it, that the 1934 Act put "a cop on Wall Street." It required that securities exchanges register with the SEC, and operate under the new agency's oversight. Restrictions were placed on margin trading, stock pooling, and insider trading. As we shall see in the next chapter, Whitney led the battle against the 1934 Act, and, in the aftermath, lost his position as Exchange president.

Ferdinand Pecora, a Sicilian immigrant, was chief counsel of the Senate Committee on Banking and Currency in 1933-34. His brilliant questioning of Whitney and other Wall Street figures galvanized public opinion in favor of securities and banking reform. It led directly to passage of the Securities Act of 1933 requiring significant disclosure in securities sales and the Glass–Steagall Act mandating the separation of commercial and investment banking.

INTERNAL RUMBLINGS

In April 1933, Whitney was again asked to the White House, this time by the new president, Franklin D. Roosevelt. Although Richard was a couple of years too young to have overlapped with Roosevelt at Groton and Harvard, his brother George had done so at both places and made no secret of his lifelong dislike of FDR. Whitney argued vigorously for self-regulation, as he had with Hoover. FDR would have none of it. In his famous first hundred days, and partly in response to the Pecora hearings, both the Securities Act of 1933 and the Glass-Steagall Banking Act were signed into law.

The Securities Act required that issuers of new securities publicly disclose information about themselves and any risks involved with the new securities. Glass-Steagall required the separation of investment and commercial banking. As a consequence of this latter legislation, Morgan was forced—in effect—to spin off its investment banking function into a technically independent Morgan Stanley, while National City and Chase had to shed their brokerage affiliates. Kuhn Loeb, having never developed a commercial banking business, was untouched.

Everyone knew that financial reform wouldn't stop here. The new Democratic majority on the Senate Banking Committee kept Pecora on, and for the next year he treated the American public to an exposé of the securities and banking industries. Particularly notable was the exposure of Albert Wiggins, who as chairman of the Chase National Bank, was surreptitiously selling his own Chase stock while publicly promoting its acquisition. Old timers were reminded of the Pujo Committee investigation in 1912, with Pierpont Morgan as the featured

witness in hearings that led to the creation of the Federal Reserve
System.

The Morgan bank was a Pecora target. Jack Morgan, Pierpont's son,
was obviously uncomfortable in the witness chair. As captured in a
famous photograph, his discomfort was increased when a public
relations man for the Ringling circus placed a young midget woman on
his lap. It was Richard Whitney, sitting with the Morgan executives in
the audience, who shooed the woman away. She would later return to
her native Germany and perish in the Holocaust.

In his testimony, Jack Morgan described how the firm's profits were
divided, with 50 percent for him and 50 percent for all the other
partners. Morgan only did business with people who came to the bank
"with some introduction." The bank loaned only to "friends of ours, and
we know that they are good, straight fellows."

Pecora was particularly interested in Morgan's practice of allowing
those on the bank's friends' lists the chance to buy new stock offerings
at the initial offering price. It was money in the bank, as the offering
price was always set at well below the stock's anticipated market value.
The friends' lists included top bankers, clients, financial journalists, and
others in the Morgan business orbit, as well as public figures such as the
chairman of the Democratic National Committee and the treasurer of
the Republican National Committee. The lists also included Richard
Whitney.

It fell to George Whitney, the rising Morgan executive, to justify to
the senators that this practice served legitimate purposes, and was not
simply buying favors. He did so in the usual Whitney style. According
to Chernow, "Of the Morgan partners who tramped to Washington to
answer questions, George Whitney appeared the most snobbishly
indignant, as if unwilling to concede the legitimacy of the proceedings."
George argued that the bank sought only buyers whose wealth protected
them from possible loss, but there never was any loss. No one ever
turned down a Morgan offer to buy initial offering shares. As Pecora
observed in his 1939 best-selling book *Wall Street under Oath*: "Many
there are who would gladly have helped them share that appalling
peril!"

The Senate Banking Committee was exposing Wall Street's clubby
ways to a nation that knew little about such things. Pecora saw the

hearings as a way to build public support for federal regulation beyond the securities and banking acts of 1933. In early February 1934, a bill that would give the Federal Trade Commission the power to police the securities market was introduced in Congress with heavy White House input. The battle lines formed.

Richard Whitney was ready to mobilize the opposition. He called together the heads of the thirty leading member firms of the Exchange to organize a national public relations campaign against the bill. He increased the number of his public appearances and sent letters to the heads of all member firms and eighty large corporations urging opposition. He called the bill "the most important legislation affecting the Stock Exchange and its listed corporations which has ever been introduced in Congress. [It would have]...very disastrous consequences...The powers [granted in the bill] are so extensive that the Federal Trade Commission might dominate and actually control the management of each listed corporation."

Washington had never seen such an all-out lobbying effort by business interests. The Exchange rented a house known as "the Wall Street embassy." There were rallies, delegations converging on Washington, and letter writing campaigns. One message from Whitney to the business community asked, "Are your employees alive to the fact that with the passage of the bill a great many of them will be out of employment?" One observer of Whitney's campaign who was impressed with its ferocity was FDR himself, who said, "A more definite and highly organized drive is being made against effective legislation than against any similar recommendations made by me."

Pecora wanted the Exchange to send its members a questionnaire about financial conditions and business practices, but Whitney stalled. Pecora repeatedly tried to meet with Whitney, but the latter was never available. Finally, Whitney did meet with two members of the Senate Committee's staff, to whom he said, "You gentlemen are making a great mistake. The Exchange is a perfect institution." When Whitney flatly refused to circulate the questionnaire, Pecora countered by subpoenaing the heads of several member firms.

Back testifying before the Senate Committee, Whitney went all out. "Any attempt to regulate in minute detail the operation of securities markets is impossible of accomplishment," he testified. "Reform should be limited to the correction of abuses and should not retard recovery by unwise restrictions." He compared the proposed bill giving the Federal Trade Commission specific regulatory authority over the industry to "the dead and unlamented prohibition law."

The bill that finally emerged from Congress did not grant new powers to the FTC. Instead, it called for the creation of an entirely new regulatory agency—the Securities and Exchange Commission. As Congress often does when faced with complicated and controversial issues, it delegated to the new agency the power to issue specific regulations that it would then enforce. Thus the composition of the five-member commission, and particularly who served as chairman, was critical. The passage of the act wasn't the end of the debate, but rather its continuation.

President Roosevelt signed the Securities and Exchange Act of 1934 on June 6, less than a month after Whitney had been re-elected president of the Exchange for a fifth annual term. Although Whitney lost the battle over federal regulation, he appeared to have the strong support of the Exchange members, particularly his fellow governors. Outside of that circle, he was, as he later described himself, "the Stock Exchange to millions of people."

Whitney's support among Exchange members was strongest in two traditional camps. One was the specialists who "make a market" in one or more company's stock, maintaining an inventory of shares in a given issue for purchase (at price X) or sale (at price X plus a bit). Specialists maintain a "book" with orders to buy or sell when the price for a given issue rises or falls to a predetermined level.

Closely associated with the specialists, and also strong Whitney supporters, were the private traders who used their Exchange memberships to trade for their own accounts. Inside information about both trading activity and the subject companies was the coin of the realm, and many specialists and private traders grew rich on information that was not available to the general public. An SEC report showed that in 1935 about a quarter of Exchange transactions involved members trading for themselves. Specialists and private traders represented two-thirds of Exchange governors in the early 1930s.

Despite this significant support, however, Whitney's intransigence, his unwillingness to compromise with Washington or support meaningful self-regulation, was becoming increasingly controversial even among Exchange members. Some were politically progressive (for example, the partners of Lehman Brothers), or at least recognized that the New Deal wouldn't be denied. Others, although Exchange members, were based outside New York and may have resented the control Whitney and his old guard friends exerted over the institution. A third potential opposition group, more numerous and formidable than the political progressives and out-of-towners, was the growing number of commission or retail brokers whose customers were scattered throughout the country.

The commission brokers knew firsthand how important it was for the securities market to be seen as fair, transparent, and on-the-merits, not subject to the manipulations of a few. The modest efforts of the Exchange to self-regulate were seen as too little, too vague, and too late. This included the Exchange's prohibition, instituted in February 1934, of member participation in pools, syndicates, and joint accounts "organized or used intentionally for the purpose of unfairly influencing the market price of any security."

Slowly, tentatively, largely behind the scenes, opposition to Whitney's hard line began to develop within the Exchange membership, and a few intrepid souls even began to work with the Roosevelt administration to draft the SEC Act. Perhaps most prominent of these was E. A. Pierce, hardly a radical, and a Hoover supporter in 1932. Pierce testified before the Senate Banking Committee in favor of limited federal regulation of stock trading. Pierce was a former lumberjack from Maine. His firm, which later became part of Merrill Lynch, was becoming a multi-branch, national retail brokerage operation focused on appealing to the general public. Whitney was so upset by Pierce that he had a lawyer for the Exchange call him in his Washington hotel room in the middle of the night to complain. At the same time, as only the two men knew, Whitney owed Pierce's firm $100,000. Paul Shields of Shields & Co. was a consistent Pierce ally.

In a desperate final effort to head off passage of the SEC Act, Whitney asked to see FDR, and the two men talked for forty-five minutes. It would be Whitney's last visit to the White House. He would spend his final year as Exchange president, and the next two as the Exchange's most prominent governor, fighting an increasingly rearguard and failing battle to turn back the forces of reform.

REFORM WINS

The Securities Exchange Act of 1934 created the Securities and Exchange Commission and gave it virtually unlimited authority to set the rules by which the securities industry would operate. The President was given the authority to appoint its five commissioners, and four of the initial appointments were well received by the New Deal reformers: two reform-minded Republicans and two Democrats, the latter two being Pecora (bitter about not being appointed chairman) and James Landis of the Harvard Law School. FDR's appointment of Joseph P. Kennedy, father of the future president, as chairman, however, was greeted with consternation. Kennedy, a major contributor to FDR's 1932 presidential campaign, was well known as a stock manipulator and pool operator. When Kennedy, as SEC chairman, called "Sell'em Ben" Smith to testify on the gaming of securities trading, Smith noted that no one knew the game better than Kennedy himself.

Initially, Whitney was encouraged by the Kennedy appointment, thinking the new chairman was too much the product of Wall Street to embrace real reform. Kennedy, in his first nationally broadcast speech as chairman—which was conveyed live to the floor of the Exchange— said that the commissioners did not regard themselves "as coroners sitting on the corpse of financial enterprise. On the contrary, we think of ourselves as the means of bringing new life into the body of the securities business." Whitney publicly described Kennedy as "safe and sound." This may be the only time he was more accommodating than his hard-core supporters when it came to the New Deal. When Whitney gave the newly appointed commissioners a tour of the Exchange, he

made sure that guards were scattered around the trading floor to protect
against physical attack.

Disillusion soon set in. It became classic Boston Brahmin versus
Irish upstart, even if the former was somewhat self-created and the latter
had strong establishment ambitions. The hens found the fox in charge
of their house. As FDR later said, "Set a thief to catch a thief." The
president had made a brilliant appointment.

The larger issue was whether the Exchange would continue as
essentially a private club, or assume a more public function ultimately
accountable to the greater community. Kennedy wanted the Exchange
to reform itself, and Whitney fought back at every turn, even replying
publicly every time the commission chairman spoke. On some issues,
such as opposing the elimination of private trading by members,
Whitney had strong member support. On others, particularly involving
transparency and a level playing field, he increasingly antagonized the
Pierce-Shields commission broker faction.

Reading about the Kennedy-Whitney debate from today's
perspective, it is striking how similar the arguments and language are to
our current national dialogue involving financial reforms. Whitney
blamed the decline in the issuance of new stocks and corporate bonds,
and a similar decline in securities sales, on federal regulations and the
fear of more to come. Not many outside his inner circle saw it that way.
One congressman who did was Fred Britten, Republican from Illinois,
who said of the proposed bill that would become the Securities
Exchange Act of 1934, "the real object of this bill is to Russianness [sic]
everything worthwhile."

Kennedy proceeded cautiously. He wanted the Exchange to develop
clear rules about how specialists operate. All transactions should be a
matter of public record. Members should not trade for their own
account, thus assuring that the Exchange was a true public market.
According to Kennedy, these reforms would serve to attract investors
and increase volume, something particularly dear to commission
brokers.

Whitney appeared on the cover of *Time* in February 1934. Elected
by acclamation to a fifth term as Exchange president in May, and with
his allies in control of the board of governors and the governing and law
committees, Whitney seemed to be in complete control of the

Exchange. The passage of the Securities Exchange Act in June and the appointment of Kennedy as SEC chairman, served, if anything, to make Whitney an even bigger presence as the battle was joined between, depending on your perspective, reform versus greed, or capitalism versus socialism.

Months went by, and the Exchange made virtually no moves toward more self-regulation. By early 1935, Kennedy had had enough. He publicly called on the Exchange to support reform, and, when Whitney refused, he gave an ultimatum to the Pierce-Shields reform group: "You people say you're friends of mine. Now I want you to endorse the program." The reformers did just that, only to be castigated at the next meeting of the governing committee. But then the meeting took an unexpected turn. John Wesley Hanes of Charles D. Barney & Company, a wealthy southern gentleman who years later would become a co-owner of the famous racehorse Nashua, rose to speak in favor of the reforms. His position was simple: Whitney's intransigence was alienating the public and the proposed reforms were legitimate. Hanes had recently received a temporary appointment to the committee to fill a vacancy, and was known for his closeness to the Morgan bank. His daughter was a roommate of Whitney's daughter at the Foxcroft School in Virginia hunt country. The old guard had assumed he was safe. When he sat down, there was dead silence in the committee room.

In fact, Hanes had disagreed with Whitney's hard line toward reform for a couple of years. He had spoken to Tom Lamont and George Whitney about it, and had met with Whitney himself, but to no avail. Hanes's public opposition was a break for the Pierce-Shields forces, and then they got another one. While Whitney men controlled the two most important Exchange committees, governing and law, a few reformers had ended up—almost inadvertently—on the nominating committee. This committee's charge was to present annually to the full membership a slate of candidates for the officer positions with the expectation that the nominees would be elected by acclamation. The nominating committee's chairman in 1935 was R. Lawrence Oakley, whose daughter a few years later would marry Hanes's son—who, as a young naval officer on a ship destroyed by the Japanese during the Second World War, would drown after giving his life preserver to a crew member.

The nominating committee wanted to replace Whitney, but couldn't ignore his strong support from many Exchange members. It contemplated—and floated publicly—the idea of doing something unprecedented. It proposed to offer the membership a choice of three candidates for president. One would be Whitney, another an amicable floor broker named Charles R. Gay who was not particularly identified with either the old guard or reform camps, and the third, Hanes himself.

It looked as if Whitney would be elected to his sixth annual term. His supporters circulated pledge cards on the Exchange floor. Gay told Whitney that he would vote for him, and Hanes withdrew from the election. Following this, the nominating committee decided to nominate only Gay for president, with Whitney one of the eleven candidates for governor. One quarter of the board of governors was up for election each year and each served four-year terms. Of the eleven nominees, eight were essentially reformers, including Hanes and a twenty-eight-year-old broker named William McChesney Martin. Oakley told Whitney, "There is nothing personal in this, Dick. It's a matter of public relations."

Whitney threatened to run for president as an independent. His brother, George, would have none of it, however, fearing an independent candidacy would further diminish Wall Street's public standing. It was clear that George was speaking for Morgan. Whitney decided not to challenge Gay, but to create an independent slate of three allies to run for the board of governors. In the election of May 13, with twice the usual number of Exchange members participating, Whitney topped the list of candidates for governor, his three independent slate candidates were elected, and Hanes came in a poor last. Whitney received more votes for governor than Gay for president. The Whitney forces were still in control.

Two weeks after the election, Whitney was given a testimonial signed by two thousand employees of the Exchange. It read, "During the past five years Richard Whitney has gained the loyalty, friendship, and confidence of all those who have served under his leadership." In December, the governing committee elected Whitney to be one of six trustees of the Stock Exchange Gratuity Fund, an insurance program for the benefit of the families of deceased members.

The Stock Exchange that Charles Gay now led was a shadow of its former self. In 1929, when 1.1 billion shares were traded, seats on the Exchange went for a high of $625,000. By 1934, the volume was one-third the 1929 figure, and the price of seats had declined to $70,000. Nevertheless, with his election as president, Gay had come a long way, and he saw himself as the embodiment of the American dream.

Gay was sixty years old, whereas Whitney had been forty-one when he became president in 1930. Gay lived with his wife in Flatbush, Brooklyn, where he maintained a small garden and was active in several local charities—a neighborhood hospital, a relief agency for the poor, the Flatbush YMCA, and the Methodist Church. He owned a summer house on Long Island, but it didn't seem to play a large part in his life. The Gays didn't have live-in servants, and Mrs. Gay did the family cooking. Their social life seemed to revolve around a small circle of old friends. Charles had attended public schools in Brooklyn, and gone on to Brooklyn Polytechnic Institute, now part of New York University. He was a serious amateur photographer. Gay's only child graduated from Princeton in 1927.

The contrasts with Whitney continue. While Whitney, at age twenty-three, had bought a seat on the Exchange made possible by a loan from his uncle, Gay started his career as an office boy earning three dollars a week. At age thirty-six, during a down period on Wall Street in 1911, Gay bought a seat on the Exchange for sixty-five thousand dollars. In 1919, he became senior partner of a relatively small floor brokerage firm that handled bond transactions for Morgan in much the same way as Whitney's firm. In 1923, Gay was elected a governor of the Exchange, but from this election until he became president twelve years later, he was never asked to serve on the governing or law committees.

In fact, Gay was elected a governor with the tacit understanding that he would go along with the powers-that-be and not rock the boat. As Exchange historian Robert Sobel wrote: "Gay would vote with the mighty, and in return they would give him business…He said little and did what was expected of him. Gay was 'safe'. He knew it. So did the aristocrats." When he first became president, some referred to him as "Charlie McCarthy Gay," a puppet for his superiors.

Gay's initial act as president was to appoint Whitney's predecessor—and strong Whitney supporter—as vice president. He wasn't much more cooperative with Washington than Whitney had been, but he was much less confrontational. When reformer Paul Shields complained, Gay replied, "What else can I do? My hands are tied."

Joseph Kennedy increased the pressure. He pushed to have the SEC formulate rules for securities trading, particularly so as to ensure against conflicts of interest. He wanted a clear separation between brokerage and investment banking, and between private trading and specialist functions. He was comfortable with the Exchange acting as the primary enforcement authority if it would only do so. He left office after about a year, with the job largely undone. His successor, James Landis of Harvard Law School, who had helped draft the Securities Exchange Act, was surprisingly passive, and a huge disappointment to the reformers. As Max Lowenthal, a lawyer on the Senate Banking Committee staff, put it, "[Landis'] tenure, however vernal have been the hopes with which it started, faded out in a dismal autumn fashion...It has become increasingly clear that Landis likes the big boys and the big boys like Landis."

Enter William O. Douglas, a former Yale Law professor, current SEC commissioner, and future Supreme Court justice, who was appointed chairman of the commission on September 21, 1937. He was thirty-eight years old and already well known for his progressive pro-regulation views. Wall Street shuddered at his appointment and some saw him as a socialist at heart. Those who did, however, were wrong. He was in the Brandeis tradition, and wanted to regulate and improve the Exchange and its regional counterparts, not replace them.

Like Kennedy, Douglas pushed the Exchange to reform itself. He called it "a private club," and urged it to put the investors first. He wanted to eliminate private traders and require the specialists to adhere to various proposed regulations. He sought to replace the current volunteer president and member-only governance structure with a paid chief executive, an independent staff, and a board that included some members who represented the public. He advocated stricter controls on short selling than the somewhat fuzzy restrictions the Exchange imposed on itself during the 1934 debate on the proposed Securities Exchange Act. He wanted to strictly limit margin trading. He pushed for the creation of the Depository Trust Company to hold securities certificates although this didn't happen until 1973. Whitney was ready to fight

Douglas on all fronts, whereas Gay sought a middle ground, not quite ready to lead a reform effort. The Pierce-Shields faction began meeting quietly with Douglas, as they had earlier with Kennedy.

The stock market struggled through the second half of 1937. In August, Gay, in the Exchange's annual report, blamed the SEC for overregulation, and actually called for its abolition. Never comfortable straying too far from the old guard, he was tilting more in its direction. In mid-October, the market decline accelerated. Most economists today cite as the precipitating cause of the decline the federal government's decision to reduce spending in an attempt to balance the budget. A few conservative economists blame the tax increases enacted in 1936 and increased unionization of the work force. By December of 1937, the stock market had given up almost all its gains since 1934.

During the fall of 1937, with the battle joined between the old guard and the New Deal, Whitney missed several Exchange meetings, including a particularly fateful one of the Gratuity Fund board, which would, as will be discussed later, result in his exposure as a criminal. Desperate for money to support his collapsing financial situation, he borrowed repeatedly in a bewildering race to borrow here to pay back there. The rumors of his financial troubles began to circulate within the financial community. The commanding figure of intransigence was losing his authority. Meanwhile Douglas was on the offensive and his threat to take over the Exchange was increasingly seen as credible.

Douglas was not to be denied. On Saturday, November 13, 1937, he met for twelve hours with Shields and presumably a reluctant Gay to work out a compromise on reform. The meeting ended without conclusion. A week later, the Exchange's law committee, with Whitney a member and under his control, sent a letter to Douglas rejecting reorganization of the Exchange under a paid president and breaking off negotiations. Douglas's response: "All right, then, we'll take the Exchange over."

In heated discussions during the next few weeks, it became obvious that Whitney and his supporters no longer spoke for the Exchange. Capitulation came on November 26, the day before Thanksgiving. Whitney and the law committee to the contrary, the board of governors decided to compromise with Douglas. Gay spent the holiday preparing a statement to be released on Saturday. It largely accepted Douglas's reforms, without eliminating the specialist function. Douglas accepted the compromise, and in early December Gay appointed a committee to study "all aspects of a further development of organization and administration of the Exchange" under the chairmanship of Carle Conway of Continental Can Company.

William McChesney Martin wrote most of the resulting report and would become the first paid president of the Exchange, and later chairman of the Federal Reserve. The report called for the creation of a professional administration, with a full-time president who could not, while serving, also be an Exchange member. The board of governors would consist of thirty-two members, only fifteen of whom could be Exchange members. The SEC and the Exchange would "work in harmony upon their common task of gradually raising the standards of finance and business." Bottom line: the Conway report called for placing the Exchange under the regulatory control of the SEC; it would operate as a public institution for the benefit of all investors.

The board of governors met on January 31, 1938, to consider the Conway report. Whitney worked to rally specialists and floor traders to declare "independence" from the SEC and reject the report. Recognizing at the meeting that he didn't have the votes to explicitly defeat the report, he argued for acceptance "in principle" only. At this point, with the vote count uncertain, Charles Gay rose to speak.

As presiding officer, Gay was not expected to speak. He had never publicly opposed Whitney. Stepping down from the rostrum into the well of the governors' room, he asked Whitney to reconsider his position. Reforms were inevitable, and the only remaining issue was whether they would be imposed by the government or by the members themselves. Whitney replied that this might be true, but he would still vote against accepting the report. No one spoke up in support of Whitney, and Gay asked him to abstain. The board approved the report unanimously, with one abstention. Later that week, the full membership ratified the board's decision, and almost immediately a new committee was formed to draft the necessary amendments to the Exchange's constitution.

Gay, honest man and good citizen, had done his duty. Whitney had little time to contemplate his defeat. His world was collapsing around him.

PRIVATE LIFE

Countless observers, then and now, have commented on how Richard Whitney, the "Voice of Wall Street," represented and reflected the old American establishment. So did Franklin D. Roosevelt, albeit from a different point on the political spectrum. The 1930s were still a time when people were comfortable deferring to their "social betters." If anything, this deference was more pronounced in hard times. Whitney never doubted that he was born to lead, and many others were content—or resigned—to follow.

Whitney's physical presence and his aloof and even taciturn public persona contributed to the sense that he was far removed, and above, most others. He could have been a stand-in for Charles de Gaulle. Most American public figures adopt a more egalitarian style, but in his biography of George Washington, W. W. Abbot describes the future president as remote and superior: "An important element of Washington's leadership," wrote Abbot, "...was his dignified, even forbidding, demeanor, his aloofness, the distance he consciously set and maintained between himself and nearly all of the rest of the world." Whitney would have understood.

Of course, public image may not reflect private reality. Nowhere is this more true than in the case of Whitney. He lived way beyond his means, increasingly financing his excesses through borrowing and stealing from his clients. Although he would mortgage his five-story townhouse on Seventy-third Street and later his almost five-hundred-acre country estate in Far Hills, thereby adding to his debts, he never cut back on his living expenses. When he declared bankruptcy in March

Richard and Gertrude Whitney, long active in the horse world, in 1890s costume at a horse show in Far Hills, New Jersey.

1938, he was still maintaining house staffs at both residences. In New Jersey, he employed an outdoor workforce of twelve men to care for his twenty horses, seven hundred hens and chickens, twenty Berkshire pigs, and the finest herd of Ayrshire cattle in the country. He wasn't one to economize on club memberships either, maintaining all of his until his conviction.

Among his fox-hunting neighbors in Far Hills, Whitney had a reputation as a ladies' man. I asked author Louis Auchincloss about this, given that Guy Prime, the Whitney character in Auchincloss's novel *The Embezzler,* is quite open about his illicit relationships. Auchincloss replied that he was reflecting in the novel the gossip that had involved Whitney before his fall. We do know for a fact, however, that for a year, beginning in mid-1936, the Whitneys separated and lived apart, she in Far Hills and he in New York.

Immediately after Whitney's arrest in early March 1938, an investigator from the federal attorney's office in New York traveled to Wilmington, Delaware, to interview Margery Pyle Montgomery, described as a rich, fox-hunting, redheaded widow. *Time* reported that Mrs. Montgomery was someone "with whom Mr. Whitney has been especially friendly for several years." A lawyer representing the lady informed the press that his client would give a statement to any duly authorized investigatory group, adding, "She is fully aware that so long as Mr. Whitney's name is prominent in the news, some degree of spotlight will be turned upon her." In fact, however, the spotlight stayed focused elsewhere, and the press, following the common practice of the time regarding private lives, did not pursue the story.

Although Whitney was certainly an active man, we have discussed how he did not appear to put much effort into expanding his brokerage business. The client base—Morgan (30 percent of its bond transactions producing annual commissions in the neighborhood of $50,000 to $60,000) plus a few wealthy friends—did not expand much year to year, nor did the firm's staff. When Whitney became president of the Exchange, the firm, although chronically undercapitalized, moved to grand new offices on Broad Street.

Something else about Whitney doesn't fit the public image he presented. He was a terrible investor, really a gambler, looking for the shortcut to riches. Starting in the early 1920s, he invested, partly with funds borrowed from brother George, in two previously mentioned Florida companies. One converted humus into fertilizer, and the other mined mineral colloids. These companies did not survive the Florida economic bust of the late 1920s, although as late as 1928, Whitney borrowed $340,000 from his brother and $25,000 from a Far Hills neighbor specifically to support his Florida ventures.

One interesting sidelight of Whitney's bankruptcy petition is the listing of two patent rights. One was for an air-pressure bearing described as "almost revolutionary in its possibilities." Another was a metal spray that removed rust. Years later, after his release from prison, Whitney would return to the quest for the next big thing.

Investors look to benefit from changed conditions. In the early 1930s, it became obvious that Prohibition would be repealed, as indeed it was, effective December 1933. Smart investors took notice. Joseph Kennedy, for example, prepared for the "wet" victory by buying shares in such quality brands as Haig & Haig, King William IV, and Gordon's Dry Gin. Whitney had a different idea: "Jersey Lightning."

Whitney may have fancied himself something of an expert on liquor. From his bankruptcy hearing in early April 1938, we discover that he owned 219 fifths of gin, 196 bottles of whiskey, 169 bottles of apple brandy, 114 bottles of champagne, and several dozen bottles of wine, sherry, vermouth, and cordials. At the hearing, he noted that the whiskey was actually bourbon, and corrected some of the terminology. One commentator said it was "as if he didn't like to see an old acquaintance miscalled."

Expert or not, starting in early 1933, as the repeal of Prohibition became a certainty, Whitney organized the Distilled Liquors Corporation, consisting of several small New Jersey and New York distilleries whose main product was applejack, or apple brandy. The drink was popular in New Jersey hunt country during Prohibition, and Whitney was certain it would sweep the entire country when sales became legal. Unlike various kinds of whiskey, it needed little aging.

For a while, Distilled Liquors looked like a winner. By the spring of 1934, while Congress was preparing to pass the Securities Exchange Act, its share price had risen to forty-five dollars—up from fifteen—on the over-the-counter market. Whitney's interest, both direct and through Whitney & Company, was worth well over $1 million. At this point, Whitney could have sold shares and paid off all his debts other than those to his brother and Morgan. He decided instead to hold, and then raise the bid. He thus missed the last exit on the road to Sing Sing.

EMBEZZLEMENT

To embezzle is to steal or misappropriate money placed in one's trust. Economist John Kenneth Galbraith noted, "To the economist, embezzlement is the most interesting of crimes. Alone among the various forms of larceny it has a time parameter. Weeks, months, or years may elapse between the commission of the crime and its discovery."

We have noted already that Whitney, as early as 1926, took bond certificates from trusts created by his father-in-law—from which Mrs. Whitney and her sister were income beneficiaries, with St. Paul's School and Harvard to receive the remaining assets—and pledged them as security for bank loans. It took three years for Whitney to return the certificates. During this time, his own financial situation grew worse, abetted by the collapse of the Florida ventures and the stock market crash. By 1932, Whitney had debts of about $2 million and little prospect for repaying. Once again he pledged Sheldon trust bonds as security for a bank loan, this time paying back the trusts within a year. Ironically, 1932 was also the year he received a Doctorate of Commercial Science from New York University.

It was time for a Hail Mary pass, and it came in the form of the Distilled Liquors Corporation, incorporated by Whitney in early 1933 and traded over the counter. Whitney and his firm subscribed initially to ten thousand shares of Distilled Liquors at fifteen dollars a share. The $225,000 needed to make this investment came from loans from his friend Duke Wellington, his Far Hills neighbor Robert Mellick, and, of all people, his governing committee antagonist E. A. Pierce. Years later,

Wellington recalled that George Whitney's name came up in the loan discussion, and he always assumed that George would stand behind the loan. As for Pierce, he may have been buying political protection against Whitney. The Distilled Liquors share price, from its high of forty-five dollars in early 1934, would fall—or be maintained artificially—until the company declared bankruptcy not long after Whitney began his prison sentence.

While Whitney continued to borrow from friends (Wellington began to feel he was "imposing a little on my friendship" because his earlier loan remained unpaid) and—more ominously—from people outside his tight social circle, he also began to use Distilled Liquors stock as collateral for bank loans to buy more stock in the company. The problem here was that, as the share price declined, the banks required more collateral, or security, not something Whitney could produce. His solution was to "peg" or support the Distilled Liquors share price—at ten to eleven dollars—by buying shares that would otherwise have been sold at below the peg. Pegging, of course, required more and more cash as Whitney became virtually the sole buyer of Distilled Liquors shares. By 1938, he and his firm owned just short of all the shares.

Cash! Cash! Cash! Whitney needed new loans to pay down previous loans. His loan solicitation became indiscriminate. In a matter-of-fact, unemotional, impersonal way, he took to asking for loans from people he barely knew. Some of these were Exchange members who were not in the Exchange's old guard and may have welcomed the chance to become closer to such an establishment figure. Paul Adler, handing over $100,000 to Whitney, told him, "I am glad you asked me." Otto Abraham loaned Whitney the same amount in recognition of the borrower's "high honor and integrity."

Of course, there was also rejection. Sidney Weinberg, later to head Goldman Sachs, told Whitney, "No," but he may have been influenced by Whitney having addressed him as Weinstein. "Sell'em Ben" Smith, earlier mentioned as one of the notorious pool operators of the 1920s, recalled that Whitney had asked to borrow $250,000 "on my face," that is, without collateral. "I remarked he was putting a pretty high value on his face...I told him that he had a lot of nerve to ask me for $250,000 when he didn't even bid me the time of day. I told him I frankly didn't like him—that I wouldn't loan him a dime."

Try as he might, Whitney simply couldn't keep up with his cash needs by actually borrowing, or by "borrowing"—as he may have thought of it—from his wife's family trusts, as he had done in 1926 and 1932, and would do again in 1937 and 1938. He would go back to his creditors, but they would offer less, or nothing at all. Some, like old friend Duke Wellington, wanted their money back. Wellington was repaid—by newly borrowed funds—three years after the loan's original due date. There were always new lenders, including future New York governor and statesman Averell Harriman as late as March 1, 1938, but not enough of them.

Starting in 1936, Whitney went a step further, although he recalled later that he never thought about the ethical implications of taking this next step, much less his earlier misappropriations from the Sheldon trusts. A trustee of the New York Yacht Club, Whitney served as the club's treasurer and, professionally, as its broker, keeping its bond certificates in his firm's safe. In February 1936, he pledged $150,000 worth of club bonds as collateral for a bank loan. Maybe he thought he would pay it back, but he never did. Four months later, Whitney, at his twenty-fifth reunion, was voted the second highest achiever of his Harvard class, behind the cartoonist Gluyas Williams.

In February 1937, almost exactly a year after misappropriating the New York Yacht Club bonds, Whitney attended a regular meeting of the trustees of the Stock Exchange Gratuity Fund, the already noted life insurance program for the families of Exchange members. George W. Lutes, an Exchange employee who served as the Fund's clerk, also was present. The trustees instructed Whitney, the Fund's broker as well as a trustee, to sell $350,000 worth of certain bonds and buy others with the sales proceeds. Whitney made the sale and purchase. Contrary to the usual practice of remitting the certificates to the Fund for safe keeping, Whitney kept them at his firm. Similar sales and purchases were made in subsequent months, and by November, more than $1 million worth of bonds and cash belonging to the Fund were in Whitney's custody.

Only the bonds were not in Whitney's safe. He had systematically pledged the bonds against bank loans to his firm and to himself personally. Although Lutes never suspected anything illegal, he was increasingly concerned that the Fund did not actually possess the certificates. Five times over the spring and summer he requested delivery. Whitney, claiming to be very busy, assured Lutes that he would get around to delivering the certificates. Lutes would say later that Whitney had been "sort of sharp...He was a man of great importance. He kept to himself. He was friendly enough, but...you could not talk to him if he was busy....I was under him as an employee of the Exchange and I am only a clerk...Frankly, I was afraid of him." Lutes's salary at the time was $43.50 a week.

As 1937 proceeded, stock prices fell back to 1934 levels, and shares of Distilled Liquors followed the trend, while Whitney desperately tried to maintain the peg. In November, he pledged $657,000 worth of bonds owned by the Gratuity Fund as collateral for loans at the Corn Exchange Bank. He also owed the Fund $221,508 in cash he had taken.

On Monday, November 22, 1937, the Fund board held its regularly scheduled meeting. Whitney did not attend, the only meeting he had ever missed. Of course, this was a time when he was borrowing whatever he could from whomever he could find. During the final four months before his March 1938 exposure, he took out 111 loans totaling $27,361,500. The loans were mostly from banks for small amounts, with stolen securities acting as collateral. There was constant turnover. Ponzi and Madoff would have recognized the situation. Aside from his bank indebtedness, Whitney owed close to $3 million to his brother, close to $500,000 to Morgan, and roughly $1 million to other individuals.

At the Fund board meeting, perhaps because Whitney was not there, Lutes informed the others that Whitney had not sent the bond certificates and cash to the Fund. Harry Simmons, the Fund board's chairman, and Whitney's predecessor as Exchange president, greeted Lutes's news by criticizing him for not mentioning it sooner. As Lutes later remembered, "He [Simmons] spoke quite sharply. He seemed to be a little peeved." After the meeting, Simmons called Whitney & Company, speaking—in Whitney's absence—to a partner who knew nothing about the matter but assured Simmons that the bonds and cash would be returned the next day.

At about noon the next day, Whitney came to Simmons's office, and asked his old friend for a day's delay due to paperwork pressures. Simmons replied that Whitney should make every effort to return the bonds and cash before the close of business. Whitney was caught. There was no way he could come up with this amount on his own. It was time to visit his brother at 23 Wall Street, which is what he did immediately after leaving Simmons.

HIS BROTHER'S KEEPER

R ichard Whitney arrived at his brother's office late Tuesday afternoon, two days before Thanksgiving. Both men were known for being gruff and direct, and Richard came right to the point. He had pledged securities of substantial value that belonged to the Stock Exchange Gratuity Fund as collateral for a bank loan and had also misappropriated a considerable amount of cash. Richard later recalled the conversation: "He [George] was terribly disturbed and aghast that it could have been done and asked many, many times why I had done it, and just couldn't understand it—thunderstruck, as he had reason to be." George Whitney remembered: "I asked him how he could have done it...and he said he had no explanation to offer."

How much did Richard need? He estimated $1,082,000. George committed to make an unsecured loan—if that is what it should be called with no real possibility for repayment—for the entire amount. He did not, however, have immediate access to such a large amount of cash. Jack Morgan, whose permission he would need to withdraw any of his capital from the Morgan partnership, was in Europe. George went immediately to Tom Lamont, the de facto head of Morgan, and asked for a personal loan from Lamont himself. He told Lamont that his brother had misappropriated funds from "some customer."

Lamont greeted this news with shock. "Well, this is a devil of a note, George. Why, Dick is all right—how could he mishandle securities even for a moment, no matter what the jam?" George replied, "I don't know, it is an inexplicable thing; it is an isolated instance, but he has got to deliver them tomorrow, and I am going to help him out. I have got to help him out, of course." Lamont replied, "I think you are dead right. Certainly I will help you to help your brother, certainly." The next morning, Thanksgiving Wednesday, Lamont made out a personal check to George Whitney for $1,082,000, representing a loan at 4 percent interest.

Richard Whitney had a busy morning. Armed with the loan from his brother, he first retired the bank loan. It was then on to the Gratuity Fund's office where, at lunchtime, he personally delivered the Fund's securities and cash to Simmons and Lutes. Both of these gentlemen would testify later that they assumed the long delay in this delivery was solely the result of back-office disorganization. Neither had any suspicion of the truth.

Two weeks later, with Jack Morgan back in New York, George Whitney asked him for permission to withdraw funds from the partnership in order to repay Lamont. George told Morgan: "Dick got into an awful jam in November, and I went to Tom Lamont when you were not here and he loaned me the money. And so I want to pay him, and will you let me take it out?" "Certainly," was Jack Morgan's reply. Later Jack Morgan would testify that he realized that the awful jam must have been business-related because "[t]he sum was too big for anything else."

Thus it came to pass that, as 1937 came to an end, two Morgan partners of great prominence knew specifically that Richard Whitney was a criminal, and another—an actual Morgan—had reason to suspect the same. None of the three chose to inform law enforcement or Exchange authorities. Their failure to act, particularly Tom Lamont's, would become a big issue several months later.

Until Richard Whitney's 1937 Thanksgiving week visit, George Whitney had known nothing of his brother's misappropriations. What George did know was that starting as early as 1921, he had lent his brother money to buy the Seventh-third Street house, a second Exchange seat, and various Florida investments. Initially the loans were repaid, but later they weren't. By year's end in 1929, Richard owed George over $1 million. In the years after the crash, things got worse. By year's end in 1931, Richard owed George close to $2 million, including a $500,000 loan originally from Morgan that George felt obligated to assume.

Over time, and with an increasing sense of urgency, George Whitney began to take an interest in his brother's brokerage business. Soon after the crash, George asked one of his Morgan partners to approach Richard's friend Duke Wellington about merging the Whitney and Wellington firms. The Morgan partner told Wellington, "He [Richard] needs partners who aren't office boys." Wellington had no interest in the proposition.

By early 1936, rumors of Richard Whitney's borrowings from wider and wider circles got back to George Whitney. One loan in particular— $100,000 from George F. Baker, Jr., of First National Bank—seemed particularly upsetting. George decided that he would lend Richard whatever it took to pay off all the loans, except those owed to him, and give his brother a clean slate. To determine what amount was necessary, George asked a young Morgan partner, Henry P. Davison, son of the late Morgan senior partner, to review Richard's financial situation. Richard managed to keep from Davison the fact that some of the collateral supporting his various loans was stolen goods. In January 1937, George lent Richard, unsecured, an additional $650,000, the amount that would supposedly allow Richard to eliminate all debt except that owed him.

George's new loan was not enough, and as the borrowing of so much from so many continued, so did the gossip. Richard Whitney also had his antagonists, some who disagreed with him on Exchange matters and others who resented his arrogance and Brahmin style. No one better fits this category than our old friend "Sell'em Ben" Smith, the poor, uneducated Irish Catholic boy who, with others like Joe Kennedy and Michael Meehan, had become a master pool operator and short seller in the 1920s. Sell'em Ben was not shy about telling people, including Charles Gay, that Whitney "was broke and owed money all over the Street."

On Thanksgiving Day 1937, while Gay was preparing to accede to the Exchange reforms advocated by William Douglas and the SEC, George Whitney met, in the morning, with his brother—whom he had lent the $1,082,000 the day before—to go over the books of Richard Whitney & Company. Richard later admitted that the figures he supplied were false, and included a much-too-generous valuation of Distilled Liquors stock. George concluded that Richard had to sell the firm and get out of the securities business. That afternoon, George asked

Harry Simmons, chairman of the Gratuity Fund board, to stop by. Would Simmons purchase Whitney & Company? The answer was a flat no.

George Whitney soon left for a Florida vacation, leaving Richard to sell his firm and get whatever he could for the Distilled Liquors stock. During December, Richard failed on both counts, and continued to borrow money to support the Distilled Liquors peg. As already noted, he borrowed 111 separate times in the period from November 1937 to February 1938.

Back in New York in January, George Whitney, desperate to sell or somehow liquidate his brother's firm, raised the possibility of Morgan itself accepting the Distilled Liquors stock as collateral for a loan that would make Whitney & Company more attractive to buyers. Once again, he assigned a Morgan partner, this time Francis Bartow, to look into the situation. Barlow discovered that Whitney & Company's assets were mostly shares of Distilled Liquors, whose assets—in turn—consisted largely of 550,000 gallons of "Jersey Lightning" and about twice that amount of just plain cider. There would be no Morgan loan. There would be no sale of Richard Whitney & Company. On January 26, 1938, Richard Whitney pledged $800,000 worth of his clients' securities as collateral for additional loans. The downward cycle was accelerating.

Ironically, the proximate cause of Richard Whitney's exposure as a criminal was a completely false rumor arising out of what appeared to be distress selling of large amounts of Greyhound Corporation shares. The Exchange's specialist in Greyhound, facing a sell-off of the stock and having heard rumors about Richard Whitney's poor financial condition, made the assumption that Whitney, being desperate for cash, was the seller. The specialist told Duke Wellington, an Exchange governor, that this was the case, and Wellington passed on the information—or misinformation, as Whitney was not selling Greyhound—to Howland Davis, chairman of the Exchange's business conduct committee.

At the same time, under pressure from the SEC, the Exchange was preparing a questionnaire on financial condition that was to be sent to all Exchange members, but on a scattered mail basis starting January 20. Whitney's firm was not in the first group scheduled to receive the mailing—in fact, it was in the May group—but Howland Davis decided to include Whitney & Company in the list of initial recipients. Perhaps Davis was influenced by the fact that he had known George and Richard Whitney since childhood and—as previously noted—remembered them as "perfect snobs" and "pains in the neck."

Whitney & Company's completed questionnaire, despite Whitney's best efforts to hide the true condition of the firm, raised red flags with the Exchange staff. Ignoring Whitney's pleas for delay, Davis insisted that an audit team from the Exchange conduct an on-premises examination. By the end of February, the auditors had strong suspicions, if not actual knowledge, that Whitney had misappropriated clients' securities.

On the evening of Wednesday, March 2, 1938, Messrs. Davis, Simmons, and Gay and the Exchange's lawyers met with Richard Whitney's lawyer to express their concern about the seriousness of the situation. They wanted direct answers to the following two questions: Was Whitney an embezzler, and was his firm insolvent? The next day, Whitney pleaded with Davis for more time before the Exchange took action, but to no avail. On Friday, the Exchange's comptroller officially concluded that the answers to the two questions were yes and yes.

On Saturday morning, the comptroller informed Whitney of his findings. Whitney spent the early afternoon in Charles Gay's office, trying to convince the Exchange president that, while the comptroller's conclusions were correct, the Exchange should not pursue any charges against him and should allow him to sell his seat. According to Gay, Whitney's reasoning was, "After all, I'm Richard Whitney. I mean the Stock Exchange to millions of people." Gay later recalled, "I wouldn't say that Mr. Whitney was pleading. He assumed more of a reasoning attitude, as if he were discussing somebody else than himself." Gay wouldn't budge. Charges would be presented to the business conduct committee on Monday.

Gay's description of Richard Whitney asking for special treatment "as if he were discussing somebody else" could apply also to how he asked people he barely knew for loans. He seemed to be oblivious to the opinion of others, particularly those he considered his social inferiors. One wonders if he appreciated the irony of his situation, such as when Walter Rosen lent him money in the final weeks before exposure while recalling Pierpont Morgan's line about how a borrower's personal integrity was more important than his collateral.

Back at Morgan during this fateful weekend of March 5-6, Francis Bartow was in charge. Tom Lamont was in Europe, and George Whitney was in Florida recuperating from an illness. After Richard Whitney left Gay early Saturday afternoon, he proceeded to the Links Club on the East Side, a fashionable men's club with many prominent business figures as members. As already mentioned, Whitney was the club's president.

Richard Whitney's purpose in coming to the Links Club was to meet with Bartow, who was playing bridge with some friends. According to Bartow, "We sat down together to talk. As we did so, he drew from his pocket a large folded piece of paper which he proceeded to open. He said, 'I am in a jam.' I said, 'Wait a minute; is your idea in talking to me now to borrow money?'" Whitney said yes; Bartow answered a definite no.

Still later that Saturday afternoon, Richard Whitney returned to the Links Club with his lawyer, and proceeded to tell Bartow about his pledging as collateral for his own loans securities belonging to the New York Yacht Club, the Sheldon trusts, and a New Jersey neighbor. Bartow asked, "Do you mean that you have taken a client's securities and pledged them in loans and taken the proceeds of that and placed it in your business when they did not owe you anything?" Whitney said, "Yes, I do." Bartow replied, "This is serious." Whitney countered, "It is criminal."

Bartow was now the third (with Lamont and George Whitney, or fourth, if you include Jack Morgan) Morgan partner who had definite knowledge that Richard Whitney was a criminal. That evening, Bartow drove out to the North Shore of Long Island to confer with John W. Davis, Morgan's outside counsel, former Ambassador to the Court of St. James under Woodrow Wilson, and the 1924 Democratic candidate for President. Davis, upon hearing Bartow's story, advised that no one at Morgan do anything to help Whitney. The legal concern was to keep anyone associated with Morgan, or the firm itself, from being considered an accessory to a crime.

About midnight, Bartow, having returned from Long Island, met with Gay, Richard Whitney's lawyer, and an Exchange lawyer at the

Having already pleaded guilty to two grand larceny indictments, Whitney is sworn in as a witness in the State Attorney General's hearing on the failure of his brokerage firm.

Metropolitan Club. The marching order was clear. There would be no delay in Monday's business conduct committee hearing at the Exchange to consider the Whitney matter. Bartow and Whitney's lawyer returned to the Links Club to tell Whitney.

On Sunday morning, Bartow went back to the North Shore to inform Jack Morgan of Saturday's events. Morgan, described as "shocked" by Bartow, supported the decision to do nothing to help Richard Whitney. Later, when asked if he knew Whitney, Morgan would reply that he used to know him. After returning to New York and meeting with two other Morgan partners, along with Edwin Sunderland, a partner of John Davis, and some others, Bartow—late in the afternoon—called George Whitney in Florida. "Mr. Whitney said, 'My God.'"

George Whitney, judging from his letters and public statements, was no more reflective than his brother. Still, on that Sunday night after receiving Bartow's call, one wonders about his thoughts. He was the good brother, making all those loans over so many years. After his brother's fall, George—over time—made good on all the bad loans and embezzled funds.

One of George's grandsons complained to me that his grandfather lost the chance to become really rich by doing so. The same grandson told Chernow, "[His brother's disgrace] was emotionally debilitating to [George]. The reputational disaster was even harder than the money. It cost him a tremendous amount of money near the end of his earning power, but he made every penny good." A granddaughter, however, noted that her grandparents' wealth was mostly in Bacon family trusts, and there was never any sacrifice of lifestyle. On Wall Street, George Whitney was a hero. And yet, were things more complicated? Wasn't he also his brother's enabler? And why did Edwin Sunderland, who was intimately involved, report that Richard Whitney was consumed by jealousy of George?

ENDGAME

On Monday morning, March 7, the Exchange's committee on business conduct recommended unanimously that charges be brought against Richard Whitney and two of his partners. The two partners were subsequently suspended for three years, but had clearly known nothing of their leader's illegal activities. The charges had been drafted by Roland Redmond over the weekend, reportedly with tears streaming down his face. Redmond, the Exchange's outside counsel, was one of Whitney's closest friends. Later, Redmond's firm—Carter, Ledyard & Milburn—would lose the Exchange as a client because of its close identification with Whitney and the old guard. That evening, Charles Gay informed William Douglas by phone of the situation, and Douglas asked now-fellow SEC commissioner John Wesley Hanes to go immediately to New York, which Hanes did by overnight train.

On Tuesday, March 8, the world learned Richard Whitney's secret. Hanes arrived from Washington just in time for Gay's announcement, made from the rostrum above the Exchange's trading floor to a silent audience below, that Whitney & Company had been suspended for insolvency. Immediately after Gay's announcement, the Exchange released a statement that the committee on business conduct had "discovered evidence of conduct apparently contrary to just and equitable principles of trade." A hearing on the charges before the governing committee was set for March 17.

The media went wild. Whitney & Company declared bankruptcy. Hanes held an abbreviated SEC hearing, at which Richard Whitney, with his usual distance and composure, admitted everything. He even used a fox-hunting term—"gee and haw," or go right and go left—to criticize a question he thought inappropriate. The next day, through his newly hired criminal lawyer and prominent Republican politician, Charles H. Tuttle, Richard Whitney released the following statement: "I want to say emphatically that the difficulties in which my firm has become involved are the result of actions as to which I alone have responsibility and in which none of my partners, none of my business associates or connections and, in fact, no one but myself has or had any responsibility or participation...I fully realize that certain of my actions have been wrong. I am determined to meet the consequences...I am, therefore, putting myself at the disposal of the Attorney General of the State, who is now investigating, and shall be ready to give him a full statement."

No whining. No pointing at others. No plea bargaining. The gentleman just happens to be an embezzler. His exoneration of everyone else was also truthful. His partners, who really were partners in name only and held no ownership in the firm nor role in its governance, had no reason to suspect Whitney's wrongdoing. This was even true of Edwin Morgan, two years behind Whitney at Harvard and Porcellian, a fellow fox hunter, and the son of a former New York Yacht Club Commodore, who was the only partner Whitney might have considered a social equal.

Next came a race between Thomas Dewey, the Manhattan district attorney, and his state counterpart, to take the prosecutorial lead. Dewey, soon to become governor and twice the Republican candidate for president, won. On Thursday, March 10, Whitney was booked at the Elizabeth Street police station by a sergeant who expressed his sorrow and wished Whitney luck. The two shook hands. On to General Sessions court, where Whitney pointedly refused the suggestion that he plead not guilty, admitted guilt, and was indicted for misappropriations from the Sheldon trusts in 1932, 1937, and 1938. Bail was set at $10,000. Outside the court, Porcellian pig—as always—in prominence on his vest watch chain, Whitney posed for photographs.

The next day, at the Criminal Court Building, the state attorney general had Richard Whitney indicted for misappropriating $120,000 in bonds based on the complaint of the Commodore of the New York Yacht Club. The club had drawn all the curtains closed in its clubhouse—really put the club in mourning—upon learning of Whitney's embezzlement. Famed yachtsman DeCoursey Fales immediately replaced Whitney as treasurer, and, according to the club's history, "covered the club's losses by passing the hat among members and selling off the plot of land to the east of the clubhouse (now the site of the Harvard Club's new wing)."

As he had the day before, Whitney pleaded guilty and made a statement—longer this time—assuming complete responsibility for his actions, so much so that some wondered if he wasn't protecting others, such as the Morgan partners. The magistrate commented, "My little experience in life has been that it's a whole lot easier to make money than to hold on to it, even in hard times. I guess this applies to all of us." Unlike his response to the police sergeant the day before, this time Whitney made no reply. A week later, the Exchange's governing committee, under his control not so long before, unanimously expelled him from membership. He made no defense, or even appearance. The state prosecution was never completed, the attorney general deferring to Dewey and stating, "We won't fight over the body."

Richard Whitney's fall was front page news for days, despite competition from other significant events such as the German takeover—without a shot—of Austria. Most shocked were the Wall Street old guard clubmen of New York. Perhaps Roland Redmond best captured the thoughts of many when he said, "I had more confidence, I think, in his personal integrity than in that of almost anyone else I knew." The *Nation* stated that the only thing comparable to the shock of Whitney's actions would have been J. P. Morgan stealing from the collection plate at the Cathedral of St. John the Divine.

As the weeks went by, Richard Whitney remained true, or perhaps reverted back, to his gentleman's code of conduct. There was no hiding from the cameras, no ducking. He admitted everything, much to the frustration of Tom Dewey, who wanted a show trial. He absolved all others of complicity in his actions. He was correct, responsive, and stoic. He was also, as he was when asking for loans and negotiating with Gay to avoid exposure, almost eerily disengaged. Harold Mehling described it this way: "His pride was devastating, yet…he delivered himself to his captors, his inferiors, with staggering detachment; it was as if he and the prosecutors and the lawyers and the judges and the prison guards were all talking about someone else."

On the morning of April 11, sentencing day for the Sheldon embezzlements—technically the only crimes for which Whitney served time in prison—a crowd of onlookers gathered outside his house at 115 East Seventy-third Street. At nine o'clock, a liveried butler opened the front door, and Whitney and his criminal lawyer departed for court. He had turned down his wife's and brother's offers to accompany him. For the rest of the day, flowers from friends were delivered to the house to comfort Mrs. Whitney.

Earlier, the judge, seeking assistance in setting the sentence, had ordered Whitney examined by both a probation officer and a psychiatric clinic, an unusual request for that era. As already noted, the clinic report found that Whitney never thought about the ethical implications of his actions. He was described as "urbane and sportsmanlike," intelligent, and mentally healthy. We will return to the probation officer's report.

District Attorney Dewey demanded "a substantial and punitive" sentence. Whitney's lawyer noted that his client had "neither avoided the law nor chosen the coward's course of flight from the country…He still has character…He has faced his friends, which perhaps is the hardest task of all." The judge, calling Whitney a "public betrayer," was not moved: "Your acts have been deliberate and intentional and were committed with an unusually full opportunity for understanding their effect upon others and the consequences to yourself." The sentence was five to ten years at Sing Sing and a lifelong prohibition on dealing with securities. With a record of good conduct, Whitney actually served three years, four months.

After the sentencing, public grumbling pronounced it too light. An example can be seen in the sentencing of a young man for stealing two dollars from a gas station in St. Louis. The judge in that case stated, "Richard Whitney got five years for stealing $225,000. That would be $45,000 a year, $120 a day, five dollars an hour. You stole two dollars. That would be twenty-four minutes and that is your sentence."

From the court after sentencing, Richard Whitney was taken to the Tombs prison in lower Manhattan and put on suicide watch for the night. The next morning, handcuffed to an extortionist and a rapist on right and left, Whitney was taken by van to Grand Central Station for the train trip up the Hudson River. A crowd of five thousand people waited to see him at the station, but to no avail as he was brought through the baggage room directly on to the train. Passing through a large group of reporters and photographers without any attempt to hide his face with clothing—as his new colleagues were doing—he entered Sing Sing in dark overcoat, three-piece suit with the usual watch chain and pig, and fedora hat. He was greeted by the warden, assigned a number—94835—and treated as a dignitary by guards and fellow prisoners. He was "Mr. Whitney" to everyone. The morning after he entered Sing Sing, an announcer called out, "All men who came Thursday, Friday, Saturday, Monday, or Tuesday, and Mr. Whitney, please step out of their cells." Fellow prisoners tipped their caps and stepped aside to let him pass. One lent him sheets for the first night.

Although capable of coldly ignoring those somewhat below him in the social order, Whitney had no problem getting along with the other prisoners. In fact, they considered him something of a hero and even sought his autograph. Like Bernard Madoff decades later, Whitney—whose victims were mostly the wealthy—was not a target for animosity and retribution by the other prisoners. Larry Levine, an expert on prison conditions, noted, "You rob a bank, that's cool. Someone defrauded an insurance company, and he's cool." One paper's headline soon after Whitney's imprisonment announced, "Sing Sing Inmates in Awe of Whitney."

Whitney moved up in prison duties from cleaning crew to teacher to greeter of new prisoners. Perhaps partly because he played first base on the prison-school baseball team, lawyer Edwin Sunderland commented years later that Whitney was in better physical shape when he left prison than when he had entered. The New York Times of June 26, 1938, reported that on the previous day Whitney had played faultless defense and made two hits for three at bat. It must have been just like Groton.

In late April, the SEC held another public hearing on the Whitney affair, this time in Washington and after extensive preparation. Here the public learned that Tom Lamont, and Jack Morgan himself to some degree, had learned about Richard Whitney's criminal behavior from

George Whitney in late 1937. The SEC counsel, Gerhard Gesell, age twenty-eight, later a distinguished federal judge, let Jack Morgan off easy in his questioning and George—the good brother—completely. Tom Lamont had a tougher time. Richard Whitney, called as a witness, complained about Gesell being five minutes late to a session, and objected to being described as insolvent, commenting, "I still can borrow from my friends."

By 1938, Tom Lamont had become Wall Street's dominant player. The son of a poor Methodist minister, he worked his way through Harvard and never joined an undergraduate club, and had emerged in the years between the World Wars as the de facto head of Morgan. In fact, a 1939 SEC report would show that Lamont held 36.6 percent of the firm's capital, whereas Jack Morgan, who had been using his capital to maintain his lifestyle and purchase art, held only 9.1 percent. In his 1937 book *America's 60 Families*, Ferdinand Lundberg described Lamont as "the brains of J. P. Morgan" who "has exercised more power for twenty years in the western hemisphere, has put into effect more final decisions from which there has been no appeal, than any other person." Lamont had a public image, which as an old public relations man he cultivated, as progressive, open, and communicative, despite the fact that he kept a photograph of Mussolini on his office wall long after the rape of Ethiopia, and the positions he took concerning public policy always reflected Morgan interests.

Aficionados of such things often refer to the Gesell-Lamont interchange. Lamont admitted that he knew Richard Whitney had engaged in criminal activity since he had been informed of it by George Whitney several months before it became public. Why had Lamont remained silent? Gesell questioned Lamont for two hours on April 26:

Question: "You did not conceive that you had any obligation as a citizen to report these facts to the prosecuting officials or any obligation as a member of the Exchange to report the facts to the Stock Exchange?"

Answer: "Why, no, Mr. Gesell, I did not. I did not."

Skipping forward, Lamont again: "I had the utmost confidence in Richard Whitney…"

Question: "…even though you had known on the 23rd of November, 1937, that Richard Whitney had stolen approximately a million dollars' worth of securities?"

Whitney entering Sing Sing Prison handcuffed to another prisoner,
who attempts to hide his face from the photographers,
something Whitney would never do.

Answer: "Mr. Gesell, I don't think I ever put it in...the terms which you put it now. Do you see what I mean? I did not use..."

Question: "You thought it was something unwise or improper?"

Answer: "No sir."

Question: "You knew it was illegal and unlawful?"

Answer: "Sure; but you used the word stealing. It never occurred to me that Richard Whitney was a thief. What occurred to me was that he had gotten into a terrible jam, had make improper and unlawful use of securities; that his brother was proposing to try to make good his difficulties..."

No action, either by the SEC or the Exchange, was ever taken against Lamont, much less George Whitney and Jack Morgan. The SEC report on the Whitney hearing did state: "The attitude of an exchange member...who fails to disclose to the proper authorities his knowledge of another member's misdeeds is consistent only with the concept that a national securities exchange is a private club, not a public institution." The report censured Lamont for "a stubborn indifference to the public responsibility." One of the new public members of the Exchange governing board, University of Chicago President Robert Hutchins, was so upset by the Exchange's inaction in disciplining Lamont that he resigned.

Whitney leaving Sing Sing on August 11, 1941, after serving forty months of a five-to-ten-year sentence. He is picked up at the prison gate by his brother George, president of J. P. Morgan & Co., with limousine and driver.

THE FINAL YEARS

Richard Whitney had just turned fifty-three when he was released from Sing Sing in August 1941. The press was waiting as he walked through the prison gate, having just shaken the warden's hand and received his good wishes. Dressed in an elegant gray oxford suit—the other choice was a standard departure issue provided by the prison—he had in his pockets $13.36 in prison-earned pay, a $20 state release award, and the $9.50 with which he had arrived over three years before. His brother George, now president of Morgan, was waiting with chauffeur and limousine. Press reports noted that the brothers greeted each other coolly. Whitney then darted back into the prison—he had forgotten his clothes bag—and, returning, shouted "Good-bye and good luck" to the reporters. He would remain on parole—and thus required to get permission for living and employment arrangements—for the next seven years.

The brothers drove to Barnstable on Cape Cod, where the Bacons, George's in-laws, had a fifty-acre dairy farm that Richard was to manage. Richard's wife and twenty-two-year-old younger daughter, Appy, were waiting for him. After a couple of months, Whitney moved on to become an apprentice, and eventually executive assistant to a vice president, of an explosives company outside of Boston. In 1946, he became president of a Florida fiber start-up that failed three years later. He then became an officer of another small concern headquartered in New York. Finally, in 1955, he joined the Jersey Mills Dairy in Raritan, New Jersey, becoming a director and then treasurer. The dairy was owned by Whitney's longtime Far Hills neighbor Clarence Dillon of

Dillon, Read & Company and the father of Douglas Dillon, secretary of the treasury under President Kennedy.

In 1961, for his fiftieth Harvard class reunion book, Whitney, while not mentioning family or his experiences since the twenty-fifth reunion in 1936, wrote the following:

"Work harder and longer hours per week than ever before in my life, but seem to thrive on it, and certainly enjoy it. Still maintain a business of shipping citrus fruit from Florida by express to individual customers."

As for family life, Whitney was fortunate. Mrs. Whitney reconciled with her husband after their year of separation in 1937 and stood by her man. Prison records show that she visited regularly, and they lived together thereafter, mostly in a cottage on an estate in Far Hills. Daughter Appy still lives in Far Hills, having married Screven Lorillard of the tobacco family in 1955. Whitney would die in Appy's house in 1974.

The older Whitney daughter, Nancy, initially distanced herself from her father after his conviction, and never visited him in prison. When she was married to Henry A. Gerry a year before her father's release, her Uncle George gave her away. Gerry, E. H. Harriman's grandson, did visit Whitney at Sing Sing to ask for his daughter's hand in marriage. In a letter to his future son-in-law, Whitney expressed his delight in the coming marriage, and the hope that his situation would not diminish the joy of the occasion. In later years, Nancy reconciled with her father, and named her fifth and last child Richard.

Mrs. Whitney was a formal and proper woman who seemed to delight in the company of her grandchildren and their friends. She could be openly critical of others, and willing to engage in political debate, where she took a strong anti-FDR position. Her daughter Nancy worked in Wendell Willkie's 1940 presidential campaign against Roosevelt, and kept a photograph of Willkie on display for many years afterward.

In better times, Mrs. Whitney had been an active member of the Far Hills hunt, and she continued to have friends in the area. Several of these, the Herman Kinnicutts and the Charles Scribners, for example, continued to socialize with the Whitneys. For the most part, however, Far Hills society wanted nothing to do with Whitney. Neighbors were too polite to "send him to Coventry" with their silence, but he was someone to avoid.

Over time, George Whitney, who died in 1963, "made good" on his brother's remaining debts and misappropriations. There appears, however, to have been little social contact between the brothers. Mrs. George Whitney prohibited discussion of Richard in her houses. One of George's granddaughters, also Appy's goddaughter, can remember meeting Richard once only, at Appy's wedding.

Whitney lived for thirty-three years after his release from prison, surviving both his wife and brother. One senses about these years his restlessness and isolation, and—of course—the disappointment of a man who had such a great future in his past. He also faced the reality that he had become so well known that, wherever he went, he was a marked man, or an invisible one. There was about Whitney in his later years something of the protagonist in Edward Hale's *The Man without a Country*; he could travel the world, but could never come home.

Whether Whitney also had a sense of shame about what he had done—whether he felt personally disgraced—is not so clear. He was not one to show embarrassment or other feelings publicly. He did not discuss emotional things. He was not reflective. After prison, he never made any effort to pay back society for his misdeeds. To this day, family members disagree as to how he would characterize the actions that sent him to Sing Sing. His daughter Appy told me that her father never discussed "his troubles," and her mother instructed her never to speak to anyone about the subject.

WHY?

Fifty years after Whitney's conviction, commentator Ormonde de Kay wrote of his fall:

> *The disgrace of no other white-collar criminal can quite compare with his: so exalted a personage was Richard Whitney that for downfalls of like magnitude one would have to look to certain flawed and doomed heads of state, such as Richard II of England, forced from his throne; or Richard Cromwell, the Protector's son and briefly, successor, chased into exile; or our own Richard Nixon, the one American President who has ever had to resign.*

Comparisons with these other Richards may be overstated, but not for those who lived and worked in Whitney's world. They would have agreed with Harold Mehling, who wrote, "As a character of fiction, Whitney would defy belief. He almost does in fact." His fall begs the great underlying question: Why did he do it? Many men live beyond their incomes, even such generous ones. Many also invest poorly, always looking for the shortcut to fortune. Whitney, however, went further, feeding his gambles and desires with stolen cash and securities. The private man was completely at odds with the public one.

Normally outwardly impassive, Whitney flushed scarlet when the judge at his sentencing described him as a "public betrayer." Was this evidence of shame, or of objection?

In Louis Auchincloss's novel *The Embezzler*, largely based on the Whitney story, Guy Prime's (that is, the Whitney character's) best friend says, "Guy, to his dying day, had not believed that he had done anything really wrong. He had been the one to get caught; that was all." It is true that, around the same time, there were a few other examples of brokers misappropriating clients' securities or otherwise abusing the client relationship. Generations earlier, Samuel Johnson, in his famous dictionary, defined embezzlers as "[b]rokers, who, having no stock of their own, set up and trade with that of other men: buying here, and selling there, and commonly abusing both sides, to make out a little paltry gain."

Members of his family, while admitting mistakes of judgment, deny that Whitney had criminal intent in misappropriating securities. In their view, he never meant to steal, and always planned to pay everything back. His business dealings just got out of control.

Perhaps, as Baudelaire observed, we descend into hell by tiny steps. When Bernard Madoff pleaded guilty, he explained that, at the beginning, he thought his fraud would be temporary, and that he would make good his clients. In Whitney's case, it was so easy to take securities from his wife's family trust, give them back, take them again, take from other clients, descending step by step.

There is, however, an uncomfortable fact contesting this explanation. There was a point, when the share price of Distilled Liquors rose just after Prohibition's repeal, at which Whitney could have sold shares and made whole almost all his then-victims and creditors, save his brother. He chose instead to hold.

The Wall Street old guard had another take on these events. They saw Whitney as a political scapegoat. The fictional Guy Prime says, "If I had not existed, Franklin Roosevelt (who had a far more devious soul than mine) would have had to create one...Roosevelt in 1936 had already decided to regulate the New York Stock Exchange, but he still lacked an excuse that the greater public could understand." Galbraith compares the way the political left used Whitney as a scapegoat for the derelictions of Wall Street to the way—fifteen years later—the right would use Alger Hiss as a scapegoat for the advance of communism.

Truth be told, however, by 1938 the New Deal had won the battle over securities regulation. FDR reacted with shock to news of Whitney's criminality. "Not Dick Whitney. Not Dick Whitney," he exclaimed. He never mentioned Whitney's name in public again. Whitney's main prosecutor, Tom Dewey, was a Republican, who would go on to head his party's ticket in two presidential elections. At most, Whitney's fall may have reduced the possibility—never strong—of some future regulatory counterrevolution. In the 1938 congressional election, the Republicans gained eighty seats in the House and seven in the Senate, but still fell short of a majority in either body.

In a conversation I had with Louis Auchincloss, who was a generation behind Whitney at Groton and didn't know him well, I was struck by what seemed to be the main thrust of Auchincloss's moral judgment of the man, namely that Whitney had succumbed completely to Wall Street's ethic of money as the only measure of success. The townhouse was too grand, the horse farm too large, the investments too much a quest for the quick and easy dollar. Endicott Peabody wanted his old boys to become statesmen and ministers, not bond brokers. Like the good old boy he was, Auchincloss noted Alexis de Tocqueville's concern that America might develop so great a taste for physical gratification that its citizens would lose all self-restraint. Despite his bloodlines, Whitney was in style a Cavalier, not a Puritan, and he had little of the patrician's reserve about the display of wealth. Of course, Wall Street works against such reserve.

Did Whitney feel life had been unfair to him and that he deserved special treatment? According to Professor Anjan Chatterjee, a neurologist at the University of Pennsylvania, "Cheating is especially easy to justify when you frame solutions to count yourself as a victim of some kind of unfairness...you are not cheating, you're restoring fairness." In *The Embezzler*, Guy Prime's friend Rex said of him, "Some of his motivations may have been deep below the surface; some of it may have been even subconscious...Guy had to destroy a world...because he could not dominate it."

Was it that the Whitneys were not quite Brahmin? Guy's wife Angelica says this about his family: "To put it bluntly, the Primes were a shabby lot, and were so regarded...by most of the people who they sought to impress. I do not deny that they were an 'old' family...but utterly undistinguished."

Was it just arrogance? Psychiatrist Samuel Barondes has noted, "If a person has this sense of superiority...they begin to think that the risk-reward ratio that applies to everyone else doesn't apply to them because they're so special."

Was it, as some have said of Bernard Madoff, that Whitney stole for the excitement – the thrill – of it? Was Whitney jealous of his older brother, who was smarter, better looking, more successful, and who had married so well? Lawyer Sunderland thought so, but I have not found any evidence that others did.

In the presentence psychiatric examinations, Whitney showed no remorse and admitted that he never thought about the ethical implications of his acts. Was he amoral? Were ethical considerations too abstract for him? The psychiatrists noted his lack of introspection, concluding that "intellectual pursuits had no attraction for him as a college student, and that his only interest was in factual material...The world outside and not the world of introspection absorbed all his attention...[he was] a matter of fact person."

A few years before Whitney was born, William Dean Howells published *The Rise of Silas Lapham*, the great American novel of business and redemption. Lapham, after some back and forth, decides in favor of honesty at the expense of his company's future. He rises morally as he falls financially. Our history and literature are replete with similar stories, but there was none of this with Whitney. Once out of prison, he went right back to the search for the next Distilled Liquors. He never had serious charitable interests. There was no paying back society, no redemption for past sins.

Why did he do it? After all these years, the answer is still elusive. Maybe the probation officer came closest when he reported the following to the trial judge:

> Contributing factors in his delinquency are pride, obstinacy, unshakable belief in his own financial judgment, and a gambling instinct...Egotistical to a marked degree, it was apparently inconceivable that he, a figure of national prominence in financial circles and one whose judgment in economic matters was considered that of an expert, should prove a personal failure...Courage he possesses in an unusual degree. He also possesses a certain gentlemanly code of

honor...*Combined with this he has a sustaining savoir-faire and a Spartan-like spirit of fortitude, which enables him to maintain unflinchingly his self-composure in the face of his present humiliating predicaments...Pride and a Micawber-like capacity for borrowing are the keynote qualities of his inner character.*

BIBLIOGRAPHY

The story and most of the quotes in this book derive from newspapers and periodicals published at the time—in particular, The *New York Times*, *Time*, and The *Wall Street Journal*—and conversations I have had over many years. As important as any source was the very informative three-volume *United States of America Before the Securities and Exchange Commission in the Matter of Richard Whitney, et al* (Government Printing Office, 1938).

With one qualified exception, no book has been written exclusively about Richard Whitney, although several have dealt extensively with the subject and are cited where appropriate. Perhaps the best of these is *Once in Golconda: A True Drama of Wall Street*, by John Brooks (John Wiley & Sons, Inc., 1969). An earlier book, *The Scandoulous Scamps: A Gallery of American Rogues*, by Harold Mehling (Henry Holt and Company, 1956), covers some of the same ground. The qualified exception is a novel, *The Embezzler* by Louis Auchincloss (Houghton Mifflin, 1966), which is largely based on the Whitney story and provides real insights into the actual man.

Two books, one recent and the other older, were particularly helpful in understanding the roles two men played in Whitney's life. *The Hellhound of Wall Street: How Ferdinand Pecora's Investigation of the Great Crash Forever Changed American Finance*, by Michael Perino (The Penguin Press, 2010) is about Pecora's 1933 exposure of Wall Street practices. The other is *N.Y.S.E.: A History of the New York Stock Exchange, 1935-1975* by Robert Sobel (Weybright and Talley, 1975), which devotes considerable text to Whitney's successor Charles Gay and his presidency of the New York Stock Exchange. An article by Alan

Brinkley, "When Washington Took On Wall Street," (*Vanity Fair*, June 2010) is also informative.

To understand the historical context out of which Wall Street of the 1920s and 1930s evolved, and particularly the Morgan role, *The House of Morgan: An American Banking Dynasty and the Rise of Modern Finance*, by Ron Chernow (Grove Press, 1990) is required reading. *The Great Crash 1929*, by John Kenneth Galbraith (Houghton Mifflin Harcourt, 1954) deals clearly and directly with the economics behind the event. As for social context, *Old Money: The Mythology of America's Upper Class*, by Nelson W. Aldrich Jr. (Alfred A. Knopf, Inc., 1988) is insightful. "Graven Image," a very short story in *Selected Short Stories of John O'Hara* (Modern Library, 1956), is another example of how fiction can inform one's understanding of the "real" world, complete with references to the Whitney scandal and the Porcellian Club. Three other novels—because of context or treatment of ethical issues—deserve mention: *The Rise of Silas Lapham*, by William Dean Howells (Tickner & Company, 1885); and *This Side of Paradise* and *The Great Gatsby*, by F. Scott Fitzgerald (Charles Scribner's Sons, 1920 and 1925 respectively.)

The following were useful in providing specific information: *Long Island Country Houses and Their Architects, 1860-1940*, co-edited by my brother, Robert B. MacKay with Anthony Baker and Carol A. Traynor (W.W. Norton & Company, Society for the Preservation of Long Island Antiquities, 1997); *The Descendants of John Whitney, Who Came from London, England, to Watertown, Massachusetts, in 1635* by Frederick Clifton Pierce (privately published, 1895); *Veritas: Harvard College and the American Experience*, by Andrew Schlesinger (Ivan R. Dee, 2005); *Peabody of Groton: A Portrait*, by Frank D. Ashburn (Coward McCann, Inc., 1944); *Dean Acheson: A Life in the Cold War*, by Robert L. Beisner (Oxford University Press, 2006); *The New York Yacht Club: A History, 1844-2008*, by John Rousmaniere (The New York Yacht Club and Seaport Books, 2008); *Wall Street Under Oath: The Story of Our Modern Money Changers*, by Ferdinand Pecora (Simon and Schuster, 1939); "Scandals: Debt Before Dishonor—How Richard Whitney Went Down the Drain and Up the River," by Ormonde de Kay (*Quest*, February 1988); *Carnegie Hall: The First One Hundred Years*, by Richard Schickel and Michael Walsh (Harry N. Abrams, Inc., 1987); *Yachts in a Hurry:*

An *Illustrated History of the Great Commuter Yachts*, by C. Philip Moore (W. W. Norton &. Co., 1994); *The Memoirs of Herbert Hoover*, Vol. 3: *The Great Depression, 1929-1941*, by Herbert Hoover (Macmillan, 1952); "Our Cheating Psyches," by Benedict Carey (*New York Times*, April 17, 2011); *The New York Yacht Club Oral History Project*, interview with Henry H. Anderson Jr. (November 14, 2007); *Pierpont Morgan & Friends: The Anatomy of a Myth*, by George Wheeler (Prentice-Hall, 1973); and *Wall Street and Washington*, by Joseph Stagg Lawrence (Princeton University Press, 1929).

Other books and periodicals that were helpful include: *Tommy Hitchcock: An American Hero*, by Nelson W. Aldrich Jr. (Margaret Mellon Hitchcock, 1984); *Traitor to His Class: The Privileged Life and Radical Presidency of Franklin Delano Roosevelt*, by H. W. Brands (Doubleday, 2008); *Right-Hand Man: The Life of George W. Perkins*, by John A. Garraty (Harper & Brothers, 1957); *The Ambassador from Wall Street: The Story of Thomas W. Lamont, J. P. Morgan's Chief Executive*, by Edward M. Lamont (Madison Books, 1994); *Morgan: American Financier*, by Jean Strouse (Random House, 1999); *The Island at the Center of the World: The Epic Story of Dutch Manhattan and the Forgotten Colony that Shaped America*, by Russell Shorto (Vintage Books, 2004); *The Death of the Banker: The Decline and Fall of the Great Financial Dynasties and the Triumph of the Small Investor*, by Ron Chernow (Vintage Books, 1997); *Every Man a Speculator: A History of Wall Street in American Life*, by Steve Fraser (Harper Perennial, 2005); *The New York Stock Exchange: The First 200 Years*, James E. Buck, Editor (Greenwich Publishing Group, 1992); *The Day Wall Street Exploded: A Story of America in Its First Age of Terror*, by Beverly Gage (Oxford University Press, USA, 2009); *America's 60 Families*, by Ferdinand Lundberg (The Vanguard Press, 1937); *Only Yesterday: An Informal History of the Nineteen Twenties*, by Frederick Lewis Allen (Harper & Brothers, 1931); *The Ascent of Money: A Financial History of the World*, by Niall Ferguson (The Penguin Press, 2008); *Lords of Finance: The Bankers Who Broke the World*, by Liaquat Ahamed (The Penguin Press, 2009); *Populists, Plungers, and Progressives: A Social History of Stock and Commodity Speculation, 1890-1936*, by Cedric B. Cowing (Princeton University Press, 1965); *Wall Street: A History From Its Beginning to the Fall of Enron*, by Charles R. Geisst (Oxford University Press, 2004);

History of Greed: Financial Fraud from Tulip Mania to Bernie Madoff, by David E. Y. Sarna (John Wiley & Sons, 2010); "Wall Street's 10 Most Notorious Rogues," by John Steele Gordon (*American Heritage*, Vol. 59, No.1, Summer 2009); and "Before Madoff, We Had Schuyler and Whitney," also by John Steele Gordon (*Barron's*, August 10, 2009).

Whitney's letters have not been preserved. The archives at the New York Stock Exchange have a complete collection of the speeches he made while Exchange president, although they appear to be as much the product of the Exchange staff as Whitney himself. The archives also have a paper, written by William R. Parsons in 1931 and widely circulated and cited at the time, which directly confronts Whitney's repeated denial that short selling was a problem. Most helpful are transcripts of Whitney's testimony before congressional committees, the SEC, and in court proceedings.

With George Whitney, there are more primary sources. The Columbia University Oral History Collection has an interview with him. Correspondence between George and Jack Morgan is included among the J.P. Morgan Jr. Papers at the Pierpont Morgan Library. There is a fair amount of recorded testimony before congressional committees in the early 1930s, and speeches from later in his career. Like his brother, George's speaking style was surprisingly gruff, in-your-face, often with inelegant word choice, for someone of his position.

I can mark exactly my first conversation with a family member about Richard Whitney. When I was in seventh grade, I came across a photograph of Whitney entering prison in a photographic history book. The next day I told my classmate and best friend—Whitney's grandson—what I had seen, having met Whitney at my friend's house. My friend confronted his parents and was told the truth but discouraged from mentioning it to his three younger sisters. My own parents had known that Whitney was my friend's grandfather, but had never mentioned anything about him to me. Several years later, one of the sisters, sitting in class at the same grammar school we all attended, was shocked when the teacher informed the class that some businessmen were crooks, such as Richard Whitney. She remembers blurting out that Whitney was her grandfather, and certainly not a crook. I have had conversations with both of Richard Whitney's daughters, two of his granddaughters, and several of George Whitney's grandchildren. Appy

Lorillard, Richard's younger daughter, was particularly gracious in allowing me to interview her at length. Long before beginning this book—in fact, for my entire adult life—I had thought about the Whitney story and sought out people with whom to discuss it. My marriage into a Far Hills family who lived literally down the road from the Whitneys, and was part of the local social and fox-hunting world, made my ability to have such conversations relatively easy. More recently, with the idea that I might write something, I have taken notes at or after such conversations, and any quotes in the book from those conversations are taken from these notes. The late Francis E. Johnson, a Far Hills neighbor of Whitney's and fellow hunt member, and his daughter-in-law Audrey Johnson (Mrs. Robert)—the daughter of Lawrence Oakley who, as nominating committee chairman, refused to support a sixth term for Whitney as Exchange president—deserve mention.

I was fortunate to have lunch with the late Louis Auchincloss and discuss his use of the Whitney story in his novel *The Embezzler*. As a young lawyer in New York at the time of the scandal, Auchincloss was impressed with how shocked and upset the old guard New York world was by the event, as if it raised questions about the justification of the group's favored position.

Three others deserve mention for their insights and useful information. They are John Rousmaniere, author of the history of the New York Yacht Club and an unpublished history of Davis Polk & Wardwell; Charles Scribner III, whose Scribner grandparents were friends of Whitney in Far Hills and whose maternal grandfather was a Davis Polk partner representing Morgan and George Whitney during the 1930s; and the late David Mitchell, whose father was a Morgan partner with strong—and negative—views of both Whitneys.

For sales, editorial information, subsidiary rights information
or a catalog, please write or phone or e-mail
Brick Tower Press
1230 Park Avenue, 9a
New York, NY 10128, US
Sales: 1-800-68-BRICK
Tel: 212-427-7139
www.BrickTowerPress.com
email: bricktower@aol.com

www.Ingram.com

For sales in the UK and Europe please contact our distributor,
Gazelle Book Services
Falcon House, Queens Square
Lancaster, LA1 1RN, UK
Tel: (01524) 68765 Fax: (01524) 63232
stef@gazellebooks.co.uk